DON'T HANG YOUR HARPS ON THE WILLOW TREE

"On the willows there we hung up our harps."
~ *Psalm 137:2 (NRSV)*

DEVOTIONS FOR KEEPING HOPE ALIVE

Idella Pearl Edwards

All Scripture, unless otherwise noted, is taken from the HOLY BIBLE, NEW INTERNATIONAL VERSION®. Copyright © 1973, 1978, 1984 by International Bible Society. Used by permission of Zondervan Publishing House. All rights reserved.

Scripture quotations marked "MSG" are taken from THE MESSAGE. Copyright © 1993, 1994, 1995, 1996, 2000, 2001, 2002. Used by permission of NavPress Publishing Group. All rights reserved.

Scripture quotations marked "NRSV" are taken from the New Revised Standard Version Bible, copyright 1989, Division of Christian Education of the National Council of the Churches of Christ in the United States of America. Used by permission. All rights reserved.

Scripture quotations marked "NKJV" are taken from The New King James Version. Copyright © 1982 by Thomas Nelson, Inc. Used by permission. All rights reserved.

Scripture quotations marked "NLT" are taken from the Holy Bible, New Living Translation, copyright © 1996, 2004, 2007 by Tyndale House Foundation. Used by permission of Tyndale House Publishers, Inc., Carol Stream, Illinois 60188. All rights reserved.

FRONT COVER PHOTO:
    Willow in the Japanese Garden
    Bloedel Reserve, Bainbridge, Washington
    Author: Geaugagrrl   (Public Domain photo)

BACK COVER PHOTO:
    Rebecca Flood, Moore, OK

© Copyright 2015 Idella Pearl Edwards. All rights reserved. No part of this publication may be reproduced or transmitted without permission.

CONTACT: idellapearl@frontier.com
WEBSITE: www.idellapearl.com

Printed in The United States of America.

DEDICATED

To Him who is able to keep you from falling
and to present you before his glorious presence
without fault and with great joy -
to the only God our Savior
be glory, majesty, power and authority,
through Jesus Christ our Lord,
before all ages, now and forevermore!
Amen.

~ Jude 24-25

Claude Monet, Weeping Willow, (1918)

I will praise you with the harp for your faithfulness, O my God; I will sing praise to you with the lyre, O Holy One of Israel. ~ Psalm 71:22

Geraldo Espinosa, New Horizon School in Paraguay
Photo by missionaries John and Colleen Eisenberg
Asunción, Paraguay

CONTENTS

Foreword	1
Introduction	3
The Shadow Knows	9
Be Prepared	13
Such Is The Kingdom Of God	17
A Berry Good Foundation	21
Stop!	25
The Alaskan Wave	27
Relax, Will Ya?	29
My God is So Big!	31
I'll Take My Chances	33
Enjoying, Not Destroying	35
Put On A Happy Face!	39
Smile, God Loves You	43
Watch Out For The Lion	47
Give Honor Where Honor Is Due	51
Listening	55
In Community	59
Nevertheless	61
Positive Overflow	63
Some Unknown Reason	65
The Clock Is Moving	67
As Good As A Fire	71
Taken By Surprise	75
Prone To Wander	77
Good News	79
Pursuit Of Happiness	83
Watch Where You're Going!	87
There's No Place Like Home!	91
Take Time To Smell The Flowers	95
I'm Sorry	99
The Greatest Of These Is Love	103
Tradition!	107
Come To the Table	111
Let There Be Light!	115
God Gives A Song	121
Today Is The Day	125

Whole	129
I Remember	133
Roses Are Red	137
I Found A Treasure	139
Bee Your Best	143
Disaster	147
Behold, I Make All Things New	151
One Is Enough	155
Put Some Teeth Into It	159
A Leap Of Faith	163
The Road Less Traveled	167
The Open Door	171
The Storms of Life	175
As White As Snow	181
Stressed Out	185
A God Thing	187
Don't Let Anyone Get Your Goat	189
Courage	191
Conclusion	195
Poetry and Lyrics Index	199
Acknowledgments	201
About the Author	203

The willow hangs with sheltering grace and benediction o'er the sod, and nature, hushed, assures the soul they rest in God.

~ Crammond Kennedy (1842-1918)

Brad, Ben, Courtney, David, Christine

FOREWORD

> Come to the table, my precious child,
> That I have prepared for you;
> Here you will find the mercy you need
> To experience my love anew.
> ~ Idella Pearl Edwards, "Come to the Table"

There is something spiritual and comforting about being invited to a table full of food and welcomed by a good friend, to sit for a while in each other's company, to break bread and to enjoy the company of someone you love. Around that table life is shared: stories, laughter and tears flow freely. Idella Edwards has written a book, an invitation to come to the table and share life together. You may not know her well, but around this table she's a welcome friend, sharing delightful stories from her life, her family, her travels and her own backyard.

It was not too many years ago that Idella and her husband, Jack, were in a terrible automobile accident. There was great concern that they might not survive the crash. We prayed along with many of their friends and family from around the country. As the days wore on, it became evident that they would survive; however, it was uncertain if Idella would fully recover. So, we prayed some more. Months later, in God's grace and mercy, just as he had raised Lazarus from the dead, and told the lame to "take up your mat and walk," Idella and Jack strolled, be it ever so slowly, out of the recovery center, bruised but made whole.

> O Lord, my God, how fleeting my life!
> Show me the number of my days,
> That I may value each moment in time
> And give You all of my praise!
> ~ Idella Pearl Edwards, "How Fleeting My Life"
>   (Written in reflection of her healing.)

When life is hard, when we face our greatest fears, when we, like the Israelites, want to hang our harps on the willows, God is able to speak into our lives with a voice we scarcely could hear moments before when life was easy and full of noise. But when the noise fades away and we draw still in the presence of the Lord, God speaks words of great wisdom and grace.

Around this table Idella invites us to come and hear God's voice – not only in the harsh moments of life, but to hear God calling in the ordinary moments as well. She invites us to be stirred and renewed as together we spend time in the company of the Lord.

> Come to the table, my precious child;
> Leave there the stain of your sin.
> Go in peace, refreshed and renewed
> And ready to begin again.
>
> ~ Idella Pearl Edwards, "Come to the Table"

Rev. Dr. Tim Ozment
Lead Pastor
Aldersgate United Methodist Church
Marion, IL 62959

Born and raised in Southern Illinois, the Rev. Dr. Tim Ozment has served congregations in the United Methodist church since he was 18 years old and is currently serving Aldersgate UMC in Marion, IL. He is a graduate of Southern Illinois University, Asbury Theological Seminary, and George Fox University where he earned his doctorate in "Leadership in the Emerging Culture."

He is passionate about being a faithful disciple of Jesus Christ, leadership in the church, and making God smile. He and his wife, Jennie, have raised two sons and a daughter. Their oldest son and his wife have gifted them with a beautiful granddaughter.

INTRODUCTION

Dear Readers,

I've always loved willow trees. We have four Weeping Willow trees in our back yard. My neighbor wrote a beautiful poem that expresses how I feel about them.

THE WILLOW TREE

I love to watch the willow tree,
So green, so soft, and billowy,
Swinging and dancing in ecstasy
As the whistling winds blow wild and free.

When leaves appear in early spring,
It calls the birds, their songs to sing.
They twitter in and out with glee
While proudly stands the willow tree.

As the summer comes without a care,
Its branches swing like a maiden's hair.
The trunk, it hugs them tenderly,
How lifelike is the willow tree.

The autumn spreads its golden gown
And the trembling leaves come tumbling down.
Their time has come, though they cling tightly,
They loathe to part from the willow tree.

Now the wintry tree stands tall and stark,
Its branches shimmer in the dark;
But oh, how sad I'd be
Had God not made that willow tree!

~ *Bridget Rossi*
Marion, Illinois

Willow trees have been the source of many stories and legends down through the years. Hans Christian Andersen wrote a story called "Under the Willow Tree" (1853); J.R.R. Tolkien in "The Lord of the Rings" has a character he called Old Man Willow; and the Osage Nation has a story called "Wisdom of the Willow Tree" in which a young man seeks answers from a willow tree.

There are many uses for the branches and bark of the willow tree. In some Asian cultures, it is believed that the willow branch keeps evil spirits away. Some think a willow branch makes a great divining rod for finding underground water. Until the invention of aspirin in the 1800's, willow bark was used for centuries to reduce pain and fever. Willow bark tea was also recommended for indigestion and whooping cough.

The willow tree is also used in many object lessons. My friend, Kim Vanderhelm, shares the following:

> Idella, when I saw the title of your new book, I chuckled. Only because when I was the director of Children's Ministry at our church, one of my motto's was, *"I am an Oak becoming a Willow."* If I stayed strict and rigid on some issues, I would break, but if I became more like a willow, I would be able to bend and move and NOT break! When I resigned, they gave me a picture of a willow tree.

Yes, there are many tales about the willow tree, but I think there is one sad story in the Bible which gives the Weeping Willow tree a good reason to weep. Psalm 137:1-4 (NKJV) tells about it:

> By the rivers of Babylon, There we sat down, yea, we wept when we remembered Zion. We hung our harps upon the willows in the midst of it. For there those who carried us away captive asked of us a song, and those who plundered us requested mirth, saying, *"Sing us one of the songs of Zion!"* How shall we sing the Lord's song in a foreign land?

The children of Israel were captives in Babylon. They missed their homeland and were filled with bitter memories of their beloved temple which had been reduced to ashes. They were once free but now they were slaves. Their captors had heard of the joyous music they once made by lifting their voices as one, praising God for His goodness. God's people, however, had lost their song. They felt God had abandoned them. When they were asked to sing one of the joyous songs of Zion, they hung their harps on the willow tree in defeat and hopelessness.

Life is like that sometimes. Hope is delicate and fragile. When circumstances dim our hopes and dreams, we are easily taken captive. One of the things to which we become enslaved is fear. Our greatest fear is that God has forgotten us, is unaware of our problems or doesn't even care. Our bitter circumstances can bring us to the point of despair, and we feel we may never sing again. Nevertheless, whether we believe it or not, the Bible tells us, *"The LORD himself goes before you and will be with you; he will never leave you nor forsake you. Do not be afraid; do not be discouraged."* (Deuteronomy 31:8) Our God is a God of hope!

I love Romans 15:13 from the Message Bible: *"Oh! May the God of green hope fill you up with joy; fill you up with peace, so that your believing lives, filled with the life-giving energy of the Holy Spirit, will brim over with hope!"* The color green is prevalent in the spring when new life pokes it head through the soil and creates bright leaves on seemingly dead trees. What a great way to describe hope - fresh, new, growing and alive!

There is hope! We may not play a harp. We may not even be able to carry a tune, but our hope in a loving God creates a melody of joy deep within our souls. It is fresh, new, growing and alive, painting a positive outlook for the future because we put all our trust in the Almighty God of the Universe.

"Don't Hang Your Harps On The Willow Tree" is designed to give you hope. Hang on to your harp. Don't hang it on the willow tree! God intends for you to play it. In the Bible, the harp was considered an instrument consecrated to joy and celebration. The harp was the national instrument of the Hebrews and was an instrument of worship. It was used by the Jews in all their jubilees and festivals. Psalm 43:4 speaks of praising God with the harp: *"Then will I go to the altar of God, to God, my joy and my delight. I will praise you with the harp, O God, my God."*

"Don't Hang Your Harps On The Willow Tree" contains devotionals, Scriptures, poetry, lyrics, photography, quotes and prayers. This book was written with the hope of putting a song into your heart (see page 127) and giving you a fresh encounter with our Living Lord.

Blessings,
Idella

Because of its drooping branches, the Willow tree looks as if it's weeping. Hence, the name "Weeping Willow". The grace and beauty of the tree makes it one of the most popular landscaping plants all over the world.

Jake, Colleen, Meghan

HOPE

When darkness overwhelms us,
And we cannot see the light,
There is a God who knows and cares,
And He will be our sight.

Do not fear the rocky path
Or future unknown strife,
For in His love He carries us,
He gives us hope and life.

The God who has all power,
The God whose name is Love,
The God who has all wisdom,
Will guide us from above.

God's loving arms enfold us,
And He gently holds us tight.
He fills us with His hope and peace
And keeps us through the night.

~ Idella Pearl Edwards

MY SHADOW

I have a little shadow that goes in and out with me,
And what can be the use of him is more than I can see.
He is very, very like me from the heels up to the head;
And I see him jump before me, when I jump into my bed.

The funniest thing about him is the way he likes to grow -
Not at all like proper children, which is always very slow;
For he sometimes shoots up taller like an India-rubber ball,
And he sometimes goes so little that there's none of him at all.

He hasn't got a notion of how children ought to play,
And can only make a fool of me in every sort of way.
He stays so close behind me, he's a coward you can see;
I'd think shame to stick to nursie as that shadow sticks to me!

One morning, very early, before the sun was up,
I rose and found the shining dew on every buttercup;
But my lazy little shadow, like an arrant sleepy-head,
Had stayed at home behind me and was fast asleep in bed.

~ Robert Louis Stevenson (1850-1894)

THE SHADOW KNOWS

One of the highlights of my grade school years in the early 50's was listening to radio broadcasts of a program called, "The Shadow Knows." This radio drama, voiced by Orson Welles, portrayed a crime-fighting vigilante with psychic powers. There were confrontations with mad scientists and evil mystics. He battled everything from religious cults to gamblers and even had the power to cloud men's minds so they could not see him. The show ran for 21 seasons all over the United States and Canada.

I loved hearing the sinister laugh of "The Shadow"! I can still remember the famous introduction that asked the audience... *"Who knows what evil lurks in the hearts of men? The Shadow knows!"* Although my name was never drawn, I eagerly awaited each day to hear my name announced as a prize winner of a glow-in-the-dark ring.

There are several places in the Bible that talk about shadows. In 2 Kings 20, God used the prophet, Isaiah, to perform a miracle for Hezekiah who was sick to the point of death. Isaiah prophesied that God would add 15 years to his life, and Hezekiah asked for a sign. God made the shadow on the steps go backward 10 steps.

Another story in Acts tells how people brought the sick into the streets and laid them where Peter's shadow would fall on them that they could be healed. Most of the references to shadows in the Bible, however, talk about the fact that, although the shadow is not the real thing, it is a representation of something that IS real. Colossians 2:17 tells us, *"These are a shadow of the things to come; the reality, however, is found in Christ."* A shadow cannot choose what shape to portray. It merely reflects the image of what is really there.

This wonderful world is a mere shadow of the good things to come, and we are not to give top billing to the shadow. Colossians 2:22 (MSG) asks a good question: *"Do you think things that are here today and gone tomorrow are worth that kind of attention?"*

Yes, "the shadow knows!" One of the things the shadow knows is that it is only a shadow. Although sometimes our actions indicate otherwise, this world is not our permanent home! Psalm 144:4 tells us that, *"Man is like a breath; his days are like a fleeting shadow."* Knowing our life here on earth is not permanent, and knowing the shortness of its duration, should inspire us to seek God's will for each and every moment.

PONDERINGS

~ How long would you like to live? Why?

~ Read Colossians 3:1-2. How difficult is this to do?

~ Do you think you will feel *at home* in heaven? Why or why not?

Lord, keep me walking steadfastly toward the country of everlasting delights, that paradise-land which is my true inheritance. Support me by the strength of heaven that I may never turn back, or desire false pleasures that will disappear into nothing. Amen. ~ Puritan Prayers

THIS WORLD IS NOT MY HOME

This world is not my home,
I'm just a passing through
My treasures are laid up
Somewhere beyond the blue
The angels beckon me
From heaven's open door
And I can't feel at home
In this world anymore.

Oh Lord, you know
I have no friend like you
If heaven's not my home
Then Lord what will I do?
The angels beckon me
From heaven's open door
And I can't feel at home
In this world anymore.

~ *Albert E. Brumley (1905-1977)*

Squirrels are great examples of being prepared.
A squirrel can hide 10,000 nuts each fall
and can find them under a foot of winter snow.

Photo by Cindy McDermott, Albany, NY

To each there comes in their lifetime
a special moment when they are figuratively
tapped on the shoulder and offered
the chance to do a very special thing,
unique to them and fitted to their talents.

What a tragedy if that moment finds them
unprepared or unqualified
for that which could have been
their finest hour.

~ Sir Winston Churchill (1874-1965)

Photo by grandson David Andersen, Marion, IL

BE PREPARED

My husband and I are opposites in many ways, including how we pack for a trip. He likes to travel light. Occasionally, while on vacation, we have had to make an emergency purchase of something he ran out of. On the other hand, I am the cautious type and like to be prepared for every eventuality. When I packed for our trip to Oklahoma for my friend, Sarah Martin's, wedding, I tried to think of things we might need just in case this or that happened. I do, however, try to conserve space by using travel-size containers for incidentals.

In the hotel, getting ready for the wedding, I was washing my hair and grabbed the plastic container filled with my favorite Pantene conditioner. As I rubbed it onto my hair, I knew something was wrong. It was watery and seemed to make my hair sticky. I blamed the hot weather, but as I was attempting to brush out my hair, I noticed a small plastic bottle containing a white substance still sitting on the sink. I quickly checked the other container that I had used and realized I had conditioned my hair with Milk of Magnesia. I humbly concluded that my husband was the wise one.

God will let us know which areas of our lives are in need of a good dose of preparedness. In the story of the ten virgins in Matthew 25, the Bible classifies five of them as foolish because they were unprepared. *"The foolish ones took their lamps but did not take any oil with them."* (vs. 3) The five wise virgins, however, were well prepared. *"The virgins who were ready went in with him to the wedding banquet. And the door was shut."* (vs. 10) Although the Bible does *not* say they had extra clothes, money or even food with them, they had exactly what they were supposed to have. They had oil, and the oil represents the anointing of the Holy Spirit.

We all like to prepare ourselves: 1) financially to meet our needs; 2) mentally to stay on top of problems; 3) emotionally to handle sudden changes; and 4) physically to successfully run life's marathon. How often, though, do we prepare ourselves spiritually?

Satan delights in attacking us in the area of our spiritual health. He tries to make it seem less urgent than all our other priorities. But if we are to defeat Satan, we must be prepared. Benjamin Franklin said, *"By failing to prepare, you are preparing to fail."* How do we prepare? Many people think it's safer to stay on the sidelines, but the problem with that strategy is that it just plain doesn't work.

Ephesians 6:11 tell us to, *"Put on the full armor of God so that you can take your stand against the devil's schemes."* **Be prepared** is not only a motto for boy scouts; it is mandatory for Christians!

PONDERINGS

~ Are you usually prepared or does life seem to take you by surprise?

~ Read Ephesians 6:10-18. Make a list of the armor. Which piece do you tend to neglect?

~ Read Matthew 24:42-44. What must we do to get ready?

Lord, help prepare us for works of service, so that we may be built up and become mature, attaining to the whole measure of the fullness of Your Son, Jesus Christ. Amen
~ Based on Ephesians 4:11-13

"So you must be ready, because the Son of Man will come at an hour when you do not expect him."
(Matthew 24:44)

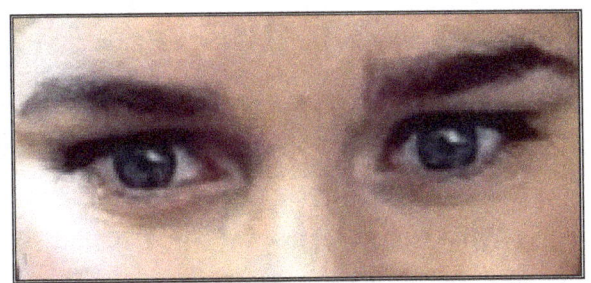

Granddaughter Meghan Malone, Fenton, MO

WILL JESUS FIND US WATCHING?

When Jesus comes to reward His servants,
Whether it be noon or night,
Faithful to Him will He find us watching,
With our lamps all trimmed and bright?

Oh, can we say we are ready, brother?
Ready for the soul's bright home?
Say, will He find you and me still watching,
Waiting, waiting when the Lord shall come?

~ Lyrics by Fanny J. Crosby (1820-1915)

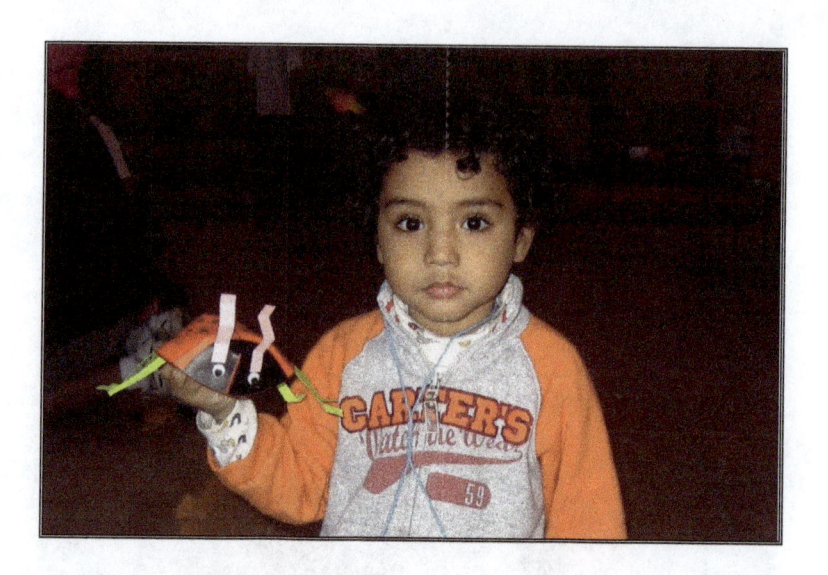

The potential possibilities of any child are the most intriguing and stimulating in all creation.

~ *Ray Lyman Wilbur (1875 - 1949)*

Photos by husband Jack Edwards, Rio Bravo, Mexico

Rio Bravo, Mexico
Photo by husband Jack Edwards, Marion, IL

SUCH IS THE KINGDOM OF GOD

On one of my husband's mission trips to Rio Bravo, Mexico, he happened to be there during the Mexican celebration of the "Twelve Days of Christmas."

Many of the Mexican families in this area do not have the finances to send their children to school, so they look forward to the Mission Bible School conducted during every mission. The mission team dedicates a great amount of time to the children.

On this particular mission trip, the team decided to make it a special day for the children at the Bible School, as well as those living in the neighborhood. After handing out a small Christmas gift to each child, everyone went outside to join together in breaking a piñata which is a Mexican holiday tradition. My husband shares the following…

> The piñata finally gave way to all the swats from the children. The contents, wrapped candy, flew everywhere. All the children, of course, dove in to scoop up the candy as quickly as their little hands could do it.

At that point, our entire team experienced a real "act of love" that came as a direct blessing from God. With no encouragement from the team members, all the children began to share the treats by making certain each child had the same number of candies. Then, and only then, did they begin to unwrap and enjoy their rewards. Our entire mission team was in complete silence as God walked among us.

When our focus is inward, we miss out on God's blessings. It is only through giving and sharing that life takes on meaning and passion. E. Stanley Jones, Christian missionary to India, believed in giving. He said, "*God has woven this principle of giving into the fabric of creation. When we give, we live in harmony with this principle and experience the blessings of the Kingdom.*"

Children can teach us to think with our hearts, and they can teach us how to love. There is no one better than a child to show us that love must be demonstrated by action. If they love us, they fly into our arms and wrap their arms tightly around our necks. We are God's children and Jesus said, "*Let the little children come to Me, and do not forbid them; for of such is the kingdom of God.*" (Luke 18:16 NKJV)

PONDERINGS

~ What are some qualities children possess that seem to disappear in adulthood?

~ Read Matthew 18:1-4. What is Jesus trying to tell us?

~ A substantial majority of the people who accept Jesus Christ as their Savior do so before reaching their 18th birthday. Why is that? What happens as we grow older that might make it harder?

Merciful Father, who grants to children an abundant entrance into your kingdom; grant us grace so to conform our lives to their innocence and perfect faith, that we may stand in your presence in fullness of joy; through Jesus Christ our Lord. Amen.

~ The Book of Common Prayer (1928)

Photo by husband Jack Edwards, Marion, IL

The Team - Rio Bravo, Mexico

José
Construction of a Casita, Rio Bravo, Mexico
Photo by husband Jack Edwards, Marion, IL

HOW FIRM A FOUNDATION

How firm a foundation, ye saints of the Lord,
Is laid for your faith in His excellent Word!
What more can He say than to you He hath said,
To you who for refuge to Jesus have fled?

"Fear not, I am with thee, O be not dismayed,
For I am thy God, I will still give thee aid;
I'll strengthen thee, help thee, and cause thee to stand,
Upheld by My gracious, omnipotent hand.

"The soul that on Jesus hath leaned for repose,
I will not, I will not desert to his foes;
That soul, though all hell should endeavor to shake,
I'll never, no never, no never forsake!"

~ Lyrics by John Rippon (1751-1836)

A BERRY GOOD FOUNDATION

My husband, Jack, was blessed to grow up with the solid foundation of a good Christian home. They did many things together as a family, which included berry picking and cherry picking. They picked blueberries, raspberries, pin cherries, chokecherries, wild strawberries, blackberries and cranberries. His least favorite were the blackberries because he said, "*They bite back!*" His mother, of course, made all kinds of jams, jellies and pies, but Jack's favorite was a plain dish of blueberries with homemade whipped cream.

One time, while picking blueberries in the deep woods of the Upper Peninsula of Michigan, Jack heard a bear snorting. The problem was that the bear was between him and the car, but he said he wasn't worried because he figured the bear would prefer the berries to him any day!

Jack and his two brothers enjoyed getting chokecherries. First they would spread a tarp on the ground under the tree. Then they climbed the tree and would shake all the branches vigorously until the ripe chokecherries fell to the ground.

Picking cranberries was an interesting experience. Cranberries grow around the edge of a bog, and the boys would climb out on the bushes until they gradually sank up to their chests. (My husband did get into trouble with his mother one time because he wore his brand new black leather church shoes in the water.) After sinking, they climbed out to get another foothold and continued picking. It would be safe to say that if Jack gradually sank deeper and deeper into the bog, he was not on a good foundation.

A good foundation for our spiritual life is of utmost importance. *"For no one can lay any foundation other than the one already laid, which is Jesus Christ."* (1 Corinthians 3:11)

If a building has a foundation problem, the sooner action is taken the better. One common method of repairing a foundation is called slab jacking, which fills the space under the slab with additives that help float the foundation back to where it belongs. Spiritual slab jacking consists of injecting a good dose of prayer and Bible study to help undergird our sagging spirts and firm up our dependence on the one Sure Foundation. This will give us a "berry good foundation" indeed.

PONDERINGS

~ What kind of spiritual foundation did you receive from your parents?

~ Read Matthew 7:24-25. Why would someone deliberately choose to build a physical (or spiritual) house on sand?

~ If someone builds a house on sand and it crashes in the storm, what should be our attitude? Sympathy? Blame? How can we encourage others to build their houses on the Solid Rock?

Grant, O God, that amidst all the discouragements, difficulties, and dangers, distress and darkness of this mortal life, I may depend upon your mercy, and on this build my hopes, as on a sure foundation. Amen. ~ Thomas Wilson (1663–1755)

Grandson Brad Edwards, Garden of the Gods, Southern IL

MY HOPE IS BUILT ON NOTHING LESS

Chorus:
On Christ the solid Rock I stand,
All other ground is sinking sand;
All other ground is sinking sand.

My hope is built on nothing less
Than Jesus' blood and righteousness.
I dare not trust the sweetest frame,
But wholly trust in Jesus' Name.

When darkness seems to hide His face,
I rest on His unchanging grace.
In every high and stormy gale,
My anchor holds within the veil.

~ Edward Mote (1797-1874)

STOP IT!

Have you ever wished that you could…..
    stop thinking certain thoughts,
        stop acting a particular way,
            stop returning again and again to bad habits
…..so that you could be a different person than you are now?

You're not alone.

There is a solution to what you're going through right now, although the answer may not be as gentle as you think it should be. If I were in the same room as you, I'd shout it as loud as I could. I'd shout…

STOP IT!!!!!
Just STOP IT!!
STOP IT! And STOP IT! And STOP IT again!!!

Perhaps those are not the words you wanted to hear, but they do represent the simple truth behind solving so much of the yucky stuff in our lives. Life doesn't just magically happen. God designed us to play a part in the way we change. We've got to stop doing certain negative things before we can start doing the positive things that are going to help us. So, STOP IT!

                        ~ Carole Lewis
                        National Director of
                        First Place 4 Health

(from her book, "STOP IT!" Used by permission)

STOP!

In Downers Grove, Illinois, I carpooled to work with a co-worker who lived in my neighborhood. Although I enjoyed the savings in gasoline, I always dreaded her turn to drive. My friend had many excellent qualities, but being a confident driver was not one of them. One of the things that confused her was taking turns at 4-way stop signs when other cars stopped at approximately the same time she did. I was amused by her antics as she sat at the stop sign talking aloud to herself, saying, "Let me see now…his turn…his turn…my turn."

I did appreciate, however, that she was a cautious driver. She made sure she came to a complete stop, and she did not proceed until it was safe to do so. I would much rather ride with a driver who obeys the rules of the road than someone who believes stop signs are optional, and rules are only made to be broken.

God places certain *stop* signs in our lives. We sometimes run those stop signs even when God makes it clear that a complete stop is essential. Carole Lewis, the National Director of First Place 4 Health, says it is time to unleash the power God gives us to stop bad habits and begin the behaviors that lead to the life God has planned for us.

In our quest to be God's people, there are four stop signs that are especially important.

1) STOP procrastinating; start obeying. *"Today, if you hear his voice, do not harden your hearts..."* (Hebrews 3:7-8) Martin Luther once said, *"How soon not now becomes forever!"*

2) STOP listening to the little voices in our heads that tell us we are not good enough. God made us, and He makes only the best. The Psalmist prayed, *"I praise you because I am fearfully and wonderfully made..."* (Psalm 139:14)

3) STOP allowing our minds to dwell on that which God forbids. *"... those who live in accordance with the Spirit have their minds set on what the Spirit desires."* (Romans 8:5) We can stop ourselves from being preoccupied with thoughts that do not honor God.

4) STOP depending upon ourselves, and start depending upon God. *"It does not, therefore, depend on man's desire or effort, but on God's mercy."* (Romans 9:16) When we consistently fail to reform our undesirable habits, many times it's because we are relying solely on our own efforts.

When we rely upon God, we have all the power we need to STOP!

PONDERINGS

~ Are you a procrastinator? If so, is it because of poor self-discipline or lack of self-esteem?

~ Read 2 Corinthians 10:5. How is it possible to "take every thought captive"?

~ In what ways are you depending upon God to accomplish His purposes in your life?

Lord, whatever comes, I have relief; I fear not danger, loss or grief. In all things I depend on Thee; yes, evermore depend on Thee. Amen.   ~ Lyrics by William Martin (1864-1914)

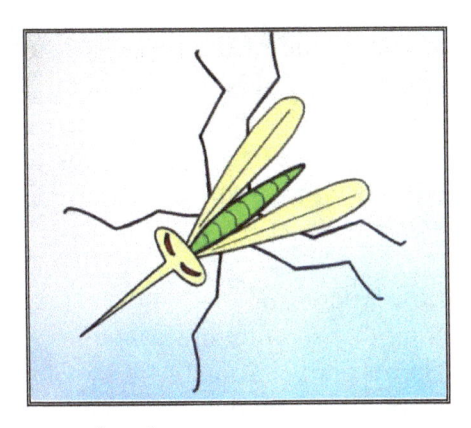

THE ALASKAN WAVE

My friend Barbara Seutter, from Washington, was privileged to go on an Alaskan cruise with her husband, Carl, to celebrate their 50th wedding anniversary. She shared several exciting events from their trip:

> We traveled by airplane, buses, stern-wheeler, small airplane, three different trains, helicopter and, yes of course, by massive ship. It was INDEED a GREAT ALASKAN ADVENTURE to remember for the rest of our lives!!! The ship went into Glacier Bay, and while there, the Marjorie Glacier was calving -which means chunks of ice were breaking off the edge. There was MUCH ice falling into the water below, some classified as icebergs, some classified by the Rangers on the loud speaker as just ice cubes.
>
> I cannot express in words how much we enjoyed our vacation! The ship was massive and beautiful. We spent MUCH time on the balcony searching the water for mammals and searching the shore for moose, deer, bear, eagles, etc. There was NEVER a down time moment. We had twelve days of every moment being one to remember.
>
> We DEFINITELY learned *The Alaskan Wave* because of the mosquitoes. The guide told us we could not leave Alaska until we had killed one hundred mosquitoes. I think three of them together could carry a person off!

Barbara's account reminds me of the mosquito stories told by my husband about his home town of Newberry in the Upper Peninsula of Michigan. It is said that the mosquitoes there are so large, the best way to control them is to install a chain link fence. I drew the previous picture of a mosquito and had the design put on tee shirts that said, *"I gave blood in the U.P."*

With all the luxuries, wonderful food and exciting adventures on her trip, it's interesting that something as small as a mosquito could merit an entry in Barb's diary. Sometimes the small things in life have a great deal of power. Someone who gets a grain of sand in his eye will be unable to focus on anything except its removal. The little things in life seem to grab our attention.

Satan prefers we focus on the trivial. He would have us lament over every broken fingernail. Our earthly life is short, but God has BIG plans for us. *"For I know the plans I have for you,"* declares the LORD, *"plans to prosper you and not to harm you, plans to give you hope and a future."* (Jeremiah 29:11)

Just as Barbara used *The Alaskan Wave* to keep the mosquitoes off her face, we must find a way to eliminate the irritating distractions that prevent us from reaching our God-given potential.

PONDERINGS

~ What causes people to have tunnel vision and miss the big picture?

~ Which mosquitoes of life tend to irritate you?

~ Who has encouraged you the most to fulfill your potential?

Many, O LORD my God, are the wonders you have done. The things you planned for us no one can recount to you; were I to speak and tell of them, they would be too many to declare. Amen.
~ Psalm 40:5

"Shovelhead," Yukon, OK

RELAX, WILL YA?

It was August 15th. It wasn't fair that my dentist appointment was on "National Relaxation Day." My appointment was a lengthy one, and relaxation was difficult. I had broken off a large chunk of my upper back tooth. The dentist said the tooth had broken off down to the bone. He also had to remove some tissue, causing pain later in the day after the numbness wore off.

It was challenging to *relax* as I lay there experiencing the whine, the grind and the vibrations of the drill with my jaw aching from being propped open for 40 minutes. To top it off, as I left the office wearing my new temporary crown, I stepped on a large wad of bubble gum on the hot pavement!

Some days are certainly less relaxing than others. The ability to relax may depend somewhat on circumstances, and yet it is also dependent upon our choice of attitude. While I was in the dental chair, I tried to think of pleasant things and also tried to remember to breathe instead of stressing and obsessing over my current situation. We make things considerably worse when we allow our thoughts to ruminate on the negative. The word "rumination" means "the act of meditation." It also means "the process of chewing cud, as some animals do." It's alright to ruminate when we are attempting to find a solution to a problem, but when we *chew* exclusively on the negative over and over, it solves nothing and is guaranteed to increase our stress. Research has also linked negative rumination with high blood pressure, depression and self-sabotaging behaviors.

So...how do we cope? What can we do to avoid stress or the effects of stress? Finding relaxation in the midst of life's challenges is not impossible. According to Jesus, there is only one answer: Come to Him. "*Come to me, all you who are weary and burdened, and I will give you rest. Take my yoke upon you and learn from me, for I am gentle and humble in heart, and you will find rest for your souls. For my yoke is easy and my burden is light.*" (Matthew 11:28-30) Jesus did not say, "*Go to church*" or "*Read the Bible.*" Although these are important, He simply said, "*Come to me!*" When we do, Jesus can reach down through the pain, the loneliness, the regret, the anger and even the stifling boredom to give us peace and rest for our souls.

So, relax, will ya?

PONDERINGS

~ On a scale of 1-10, where is your stress level? What things contribute to higher stress?

~ Read Matthew 6:31-34. Worry has been called the American pastime. Is this true in your life? What does this Scripture tell us?

~ Are you too stressed to be blessed? Or too blessed to be stressed? How does counting your blessings relieve stress?

Jesus, the very thought of Thee, with sweetness fills my breast. But sweeter far Thy face to see, and in Thy presence rest. Amen.
~ Lyrics by Bernard of Clairvaux (1090-1153)

Granddaughter Christine Andersen,
with children at First Baptist Church, Marion, IL

MY GOD IS SO BIG!

I love children's choirs! One Sunday, our grandkids sang a song at their church with the other children, complete with great enthusiasm and motions, telling about the greatness of God. They sang: *"My God is so big, so strong and so mighty. There's nothing my God cannot do!"* Children seem to grasp this truth more quickly than adults. They have no doubt that the song is true. We, as adults, verbally express a similar belief, and yet sometimes, deep in our hearts, doubt begins to creep in. We allow it to cloud our faith in a limitless God because, in our finite minds, some situations appear to be impossible.

One time, in Ohio, my husband was out of a job for a length of time, and the bills were beginning to pile up. He was finally offered an engineering job with a generous salary but was uncomfortable accepting a position with a beer brewery. We decided to decline the offer and trust God. The very next week, he was offered a job as an engineer with Columbia Gas, which he accepted. God loves us, and He is big enough to meet our needs. The word "impossible" is not in God's vocabulary.

One great example of God's power is the Bible story of the 10 plagues of Egypt. In the 8th chapter of Exodus, before the 3rd plague, God warned Pharaoh: *"If you do not let my people go, I will send swarms of flies on you and your officials, on your people and into your houses."* God's power became even clearer when he allowed the plagues to fall on the Egyptians, but not on the Israelites. God said, *"But on that day I will deal differently with the land of Goshen, where my people live; no swarms of flies will be there, so that you will know that I, the LORD, am in this land."* (Exodus 8:22) Did you ever have two flies in the house and tell one to stay in one room and one to stay in the other? God, however, was in complete control of the swarms of flies in Egypt.

"There's nothing my God cannot do!" God's power can raise us up above our circumstances. God's power can comfort us when we are fearful or alone. God's power can protect us from Satan's deceptive schemes. God's power can fill us with joy when there is no earthly reason to be joyful.

With God, nothing is impossible. In Luke, Chapter 1, Mary questioned the angel about the prophecy, *"How will this be...since I am a virgin?"* (vs. 34) The angel answered her, *"Nothing is impossible with God!"* (vs. 37) Remember! *"My God is so big, so strong and so mighty! There's nothing my God cannot do!"*

PONDERINGS

~ Read Ephesians 3:20. According to this verse, what is God able to do? How would you evaluate your prayers with this in mind?

~ A.W. Tozer said, *"What comes into our mind when we think about God is the most important thing about us."* Do you agree?

~ Read 1 Chronicles 29:11-13. How do these verses make you feel about God?

O Sovereign LORD, you have begun to show to your servant your greatness and your strong hand. For what god is there in heaven or on earth who can do the deeds and mighty works you do? Amen.
~ Deuteronomy 3:24

Granddaughter Christine Andersen, Marion, IL

I'LL TAKE MY CHANCES

I've never been, nor ever will be, a gambler. Yet as "luck" would have it, we lived in Las Vegas for three years. My husband had a great job with the State of Nevada as a Senior Engineering Analyst, and we met some wonderful people there. One thing, however, that was hard to get accustomed to was the presence of slot machines inside the entrances of all the grocery stores. There were always several shoppers using the machines with a full cart of groceries parked beside them. (Perhaps they made their purchases first to ensure they didn't gamble away their grocery money.)

I worked for a law firm in Las Vegas. One of my co-workers would drop her mother off at the nickel slots every morning, five days a week and pick her up in the evening after work. We observed many instances where some of the local people were just as drawn to the lure of the "one-armed bandits" as the visitors were. More than 100 Gamblers Anonymous meetings are offered throughout the city each week.

Why do people gamble? Why do they risk losing the money they need for rent, baby formula or even medicine? Of course the problem is not restricted to Las Vegas. There are those who become addicted to purchasing lottery tickets even though the odds of winning the Mega Millions is probably 600 times worse than being struck by lightning. People are not really paying for the chance; they are paying for the dream. They fantasize that all their financial worries will be over if they could just win the lottery.

We are all gamblers, whether or not we ever put a coin in a slot machine or buy a lottery ticket. Sometimes, we are content to take our chances. We ignore bad habits that jeopardize our health, finances, relationships and even our spiritual growth.

Louis Pasteur was a French chemist and biologist, who became famous for his contributions to medicine and industry. During his research, he encountered many challenging problems and was ridiculed by the scientific community. He said: "*Let me tell you the secret that has led me to my goal. My strength lies solely in my tenacity.*" He never gave up! How would you rate YOUR tenacity?

In 2 Chronicles 15, the King of Judah was given advice: "*But as for you, be strong and do not give up, for your work will be rewarded.*" When King Asa heard these words, he took courage. Knowing that God will richly reward us for our hard work gives us the courage we need to tenaciously reach for our goal.

The next time you are tempted to say, "*I'll take my chances,*" consider this: the easy pathway usually does not take us where we want to go.

PONDERINGS

~ In what areas of life do you tend to "take your chances"?

~ How would you rate your tenacity? Why?

~ Read Galatians 6:9. What kind of harvest is it talking about?

O gracious and holy Father, give us wisdom to perceive you, diligence to seek you, patience to wait for you, eyes to behold you, a heart to meditate upon you, and a life to proclaim you; through the power of the Spirit of Jesus Christ, our Lord. Amen

~ Saint Benedict (480–547)

Turkey by granddaughter Christine Andersen, Marion, IL

ENJOYING, NOT DESTROYING
By daughter, Kerry Jo Montoya, Yukon, Oklahoma

Shocking as it may seem, I've lost 48 pounds over the past 4-5 years. Does it depress me that only my doctor and I can tell I've lost half a person in weight? Okay, half of a 96 pound weakling, but STILL!!

BUT with these last pounds, gained and lost many times, I've come to realize one thing; it's a pivotal point for me. No, it doesn't suddenly launch me into the world's most beautiful status. However, gaining and losing these pounds so many times have allowed me to recognize that this weight makes a BIG difference in how I feel.

Now I'm not foolish enough to believe I'll never feel bloated again. Nor am I foolish enough to believe I'll no longer have setbacks, but I can take a moment and recognize this milestone. I can take a moment to enjoy that my clothes fit better, that I have more energy, that my mind is clearer and that, at least for now, I don't feel bloated! As I persevere I can look back at this moment, look at the previous years that lacked this difference and realize that even when life seems hopeless, even when it seems too hard, change IS coming if I just keep striving. Maybe the next 5 pounds will be just as pivotal, or maybe it'll take another 48, but one day, somehow, I will reach my next milestone, and until then I can carry this memory with me.

So remember, whatever you're facing in life, however daunting it seems, however long it continues, if you persevere, change WILL come. If you get discouraged by how often you fail, discouraged when you take a step forward only to get knocked back two, maybe, just maybe, God is letting you relive this enough times to recognize the turning point that it truly is. Maybe He's allowing you to fully cement this accomplishment in your head because it will carry you forward. And just maybe it will provide you with the joy that it provides me.

This Thanksgiving, I'll be doing what matters more to me than anything. I'll be traveling to see my beloved family. In fact, I'm going to meet NEW family! How wonderful is that? This year, with my joyous milestone, even with the plethora of food that accommodates this holiday, I'll be able to enjoy myself without destroying myself. This holiday's food is a far second to the joy of spending time with my folks.

At the time of this printing, Kerry has lost enough weight that she no longer needs medicine for blood pressure, cholesterol or diabetes!

PONDERINGS

~ What are some things people enjoy that can be destructive?

~ Read 1 John 2:15-17. What does this Scripture mean by "the world" or "the things in the world"?

~ What should we do if we find our love of the world growing?

Fill my cup, Lord; I lift it up, Lord! Come and quench this thirsting of my soul. Bread of heaven, feed me till I want no more. Fill my cup, fill it up and make me whole! Amen.
~ Lyrics by Richard Eugene Blanchard, Sr. (1925-2004)

GOD'S GIFT OF FAMILY

It's time for the holidays once again…
That magical time of year
When family and friends gather together;
Traveling from far and near.

Amid the cries of, "My, how you've grown!"
And, "I wish you lived nearby!"…
We can't seem to get enough hugs all around
As tears of joy fill the eye.

A time to enjoy the wee little ones;
Each cuddly body on a lap,
And big, round, soft saucer eyes all pleading
To get out of taking a nap.

A time for the older children to perform
A song or a dance they know.
The eyes of adults all shine with pride
As they enjoy the show.

A time for Great-Grandma to tickle the ivories
With nimble, racing fingers;
Everyone singing along with great gusto
While around the piano they linger.

A time to recall events of the past,
Talking far into the night.
Laughter rolls through the house like a wave,
Splashing each one with delight.

And last, but not least, a time to remember
That our Awesome God above
Blesses our lives with family and friends
As a token of His great love!

~ *Idella Pearl Edwards*

If you want happiness for an hour
    - take a nap.
If you want happiness for a day
    - go fishing.
If you want happiness for a year
    - inherit a fortune.
If you want happiness for a lifetime
    - help someone else.

~ Chinese Proverb

Tom Silver and friends in Alaska

PUT ON A HAPPY FACE!

I reconnected via email and Facebook, with several members of my high school graduating class (Class of 1957 - East Aurora, Illinois.) One of my classmates, Tom Silver, shared the following story with me.

> In July of 1999, we tent camped and rafted the Tatshenshini River from Haines Junction, Yukon Territory, through British Columbia (B.C.), Canada. Through Alaska to Dry Bay on the Pacific Ocean, we had two rafts, one inflatable kayak, 11 friends (5 women and 6 men) with two guides for our 2-week adventure. All were B.C. Canadians, except me, of course.
>
> I had NO idea what I was biting off... St. Elias Mountain Range peaks soaring to over 18,000 feet, immense glacier trains calving into our river, a one-hour run of roaring whitewater and a near disaster - lost an oar, one man overboard (rescued by our trailing raft #2), rotating storm cells providing wind-driven sleets and glacier cold river drafts. The Tatshenshini River provides access to a surreal scenery with a magnitude that few humans will ever witness; over 13,000,000 acres (nearly six Yellowstone Parks!) of Wrangell-St. Elias National Park and Preserve.

Our five B.C. Canadian women (ages 25 - 69) were plenty tough enough to do daily camp chores, yet cheerful from breakfast to sunset. I whined at Day 11 breakfast and was promptly scolded by Suzanne for being "snarky." I promptly changed my attitude and put on a happy face.

I'm sure Tom had several legitimate reasons for whining. I cannot imagine myself in that same situation. It's easy to become an accomplished whiner but much more difficult to put on a happy face during trying circumstances. Philippians 2:14, 15 tells us to: *"Do everything without complaining or arguing, so that you may become blameless and pure, children of God without fault in a crooked and depraved generation, in which you shine like stars in the universe."* That's a pretty big order: To do EVERYTHING without grumbling! To SHINE LIKE STARS in the universe, however, is an even bigger challenge.

My friend Tom made it sound pretty simple. He said, "*I promptly changed my attitude and put on a happy face.*" He made the choice to stop whining and start being grateful. 1 Thessalonians 5:18 tells us to *"give thanks in ALL circumstances, for this is God's will for you in Christ Jesus."* The choice is ours, and whether or not we *shine like stars in the universe* may depend upon our choice.

PONDERINGS

~ Read James 1:2-4. How is God's perspective on the trials we face different from ours?

~ Is thankfulness lacking in our culture? Where do you see a lack of thankfulness the most?

~ Why do you think it is easier to whine and complain than to be grateful?

O Lord of heaven and earth and sea; to Thee all praise and glory be. How shall we show our love to Thee, who givest all? Amen.
~ Christopher Wordsworth, (1807-1885)

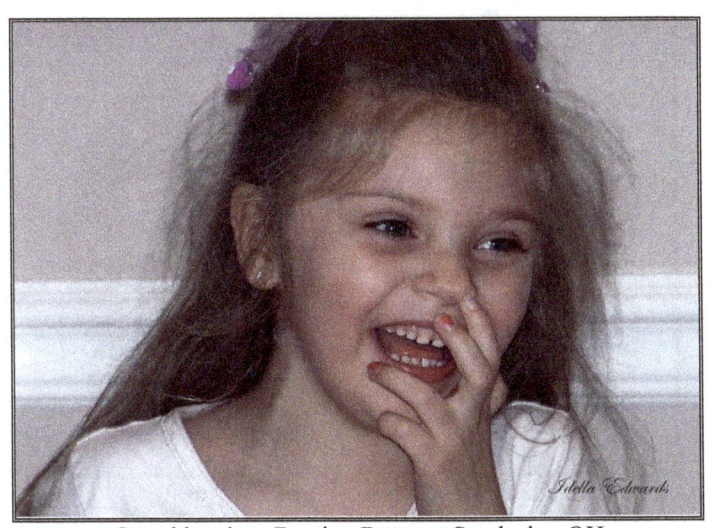

Granddaughter Destiny Benson, Sandusky, OH

CHOOSE TO BE HAPPY

How can I choose to be happy
When the world around me is crumbling?
How can I smile and dance and sing
When my feet are sore from stumbling?

The sun will eventually shine…
Will my strength and stamina last?
Will Your strong, mighty arms undergird me again
As they have done in the past?

My happiness lies in submission,
In knowing that You know best.
O Giver of Life, Creator of Joy,
Help me to know that I'm blessed!

I choose, O Lord, to be happy
In all I say and do.
You're all I need, both now and forever;
My joy, O Lord, is in You!

~ Idella Pearl Edwards

> A person without a sense of humor is like a wagon without springs.
>
> It's jolted by every pebble on the road.
>
> ~ Henry Ward Beecher

Granddaughter Jackie Edwards, Everson, WA

THE BIG YELLOW BOOK

Oh, no! She's coming! Where can I hide?
In her eyes she has "that look."
My granddaughter is coming and, in her hand,
Is the great big yellow book!

It matters not that I'm trying my hardest
To put a meal on the table while it's hot;
With a grin on her face, she begins to read
From the big yellow book without stop.

Though I plead, "I am too busy now,"
She says it will just take a minute;
Then she reads joke after joke after joke;
I should not have let her begin it!

But I notice a twinkle in her eyes of blue
As she manages to make me smile;
She successfully tickled my funny bone,
And I am sure we will eat after while.

So if a teenager comes your way,
And you notice she has "that look,"
You have no choice, get ready to smile
As she reads from the big yellow book.

~ *Idella Pearl Edwards*

SMILE, GOD LOVES YOU

How important is it to find humor in our world? We all love smiling faces, and as you can tell by the collection above, I also like *smiley faces*.

The expression on our face is affected by our mood, but our mood can also be directly affected by our facial expressions. If you make the choice to frown all day, you will most likely be miserable. If you force yourself to smile, you're more likely to enjoy yourself. According to Proverbs 17:22, a smile may even be good medicine. *"A cheerful disposition is good for your health; gloom and doom leave you bone-tired.!"* (MSG)

There are probably a couple things about smiles you didn't know. 1) It may make you smarter! In one study, people who smiled during a test performed better. 2) It might add years to your life! In another study, scientists looked at pictures of baseball players taken in 1952. They discovered that the ones who smiled when they had their pictures taken lived an average of seven years longer.

My husband and I were coordinators of Lay Witness Missions through the United Methodist Church for over 20 years. One of the first things we did was ask everyone to turn to the person next to them and say, *"Smile, God loves you and so do I."* Then we told them, *"If you have trouble saying that, turn to them and say...Smile, God loves you and I'm trying."*

Jesus wants each of us to put a smile on our face, but He is even more concerned that we have joy in our hearts. He said. *"I have told you this so that my joy may be in you and that your joy may be complete."* (John 15:11) There is a difference between happiness and joy. Depending on the translation, the words "happy" and "happiness" appear in the Bible about 30 times. "Joy" and "rejoice" are found over 300 times.

How do we obtain joy? Where do we find it? Joy can be elusive when we are searching for it, especially if we are looking in all the wrong places. Galatians 5:22-23 tells us that joy is a fruit of the Spirit, *"The fruit of the Spirit is love, joy, peace, patience, kindness, goodness, faithfulness, gentleness and self-control."* This verse tells us that joy comes from God's Spirit, and that it is a by-product like a fruit. It's necessary to invite the Spirit into our lives for the fruit to develop. If we grow our roots into God's fertile soil and water with God's Word and obedience, joy is a natural result.

St. Augustine (354-430) once said, *"God loves each of us as if there were only one of us."* So... SMILE, GOD LOVES YOU!

PONDERINGS

~ Statistics show that kids smile 400 times a day and adults 20 times a day. Why the big difference?

~ How do our experiences with human love shape our view of God's love?

~ What makes you smile the most?

Grant to us, O Lord, the royalty of inward happiness. Daily renew in us the sense of joy, and let the eternal spirit of the Father dwell in our souls. Amen.   ~ Robert Louis Stevenson (1850–1894)

LOVE LETTER FROM GOD

Dear child, I loved you with an everlasting love
Before the world began;
Before the creation of time and space,
You were part of My master plan.

I know each and every problem you have;
I know you are longing to be free;
But as you go through each tribulation,
Where do you think I'll be?

I'll be beside you, holding your hand,
Leading you toward the light;
I'll give you the strength, I'll give you the courage
To face the darkest night.

Do not tolerate the scorpions of fear
That scurry at your feet;
For I give you power to trample them,
And cause them to retreat.

My precious child, I give you My peace
To wrap around your soul;
Rest your spirit in My power and love,
For I am in control.

~ Idella Pearl Edwards

Maasai Mara, Kenya

Hwange National Park, Zimbabwe

Maasai Mara, Kenya
Photos by cousin Ziden L. Nutt, Carthage, MO

Oil Painting by Idella Edwards

WATCH OUT FOR THE LION

Lions and other big cats are fascinating to watch. When my husband worked for the Public Service Commission in Las Vegas during the late 80's, we visited the Lion Habitat at the MGM Grand. It was a 5,000 square-foot jungle where the public can view lions at play behind protective glass. It included rocks, trees and plenty of lion "toys." Visitors could have their picture taken (for a fee) with four-month-old lion cubs. Also, the Mirage Hotel had a white tiger show that was very popular at that time.

Watching lions at play behind protective glass or watching a trainer frolic with a live tiger can give a false sense of security. The animals look soft and cuddly and act much like housecats in their antics. Lions, however, are fierce predators and can weigh well over 600 pounds. I would not want to meet one in my backyard.

Meeting a lion in the backyard is exactly what one of the residents did during our stay in Las Vegas. A woman went outside one morning to take out the trash only to discover a mountain lion perched on the cement wall behind her home. She quickly re-entered the house and called the Department of Wildlife. She was immensely relieved when they captured the animal.

1 Peter 5:8 tells us to, "*Be self-controlled and alert. Your enemy the devil prowls around like a roaring lion looking for someone to devour.*" Notice that Satan does not announce his coming...he prowls. Don't expect him to bare his teeth and roar. He may even look cuddly and playful. The Bible says that "*Satan himself masquerades as an angel of light.*" (2 Corinthians 11:14)

The best way to spot him is simple. He will be the one who tempts us to ignore God's commands and entices us to doubt God's love.

When our enemy makes us an offer, he makes it appear desirable and permissible. Satan enjoys presenting half-truths, mixed in with just enough truth to make it acceptable. I love the words of the Apostle Paul in 1 Corinthians 6:12: "*Everything is permissible for me - but not everything is beneficial. Everything is permissible for me - but I will not be mastered by anything.*"

If we are to be "self-controlled and alert," we must not be lulled into complacency by Satan's deceptions. You will hear his voice saying..."*There's no need to do that now - you have plenty of time*"..."*Just one won't hurt*"..."*You've had a hard day - you deserve that*"..."*You've failed so many times - why even try?*"..."*Life is short, so if it feels good, do it.*"

Watch out for the lion!

PONDERINGS

~ Read 1 Peter 5:8. Peter tells us to be self-controlled and alert but never encourages us to be fearful. Should we be?

~ How does Satan influence people? Directly? Indirectly?

~ Read Matthew 4:1-4. Is Satan powerless against God's word? What tactics does he use to confuse us?

Lord, defend us from all dangers and adversities; and be graciously pleased to take us, and all who are dear to us, under your fatherly care and protection. Amen.   ~ Book of Common Prayer (1928)

"This lion charged me in the Zambezi area of Zimbabwe. Like Satan, it had quietly worked its way around within 30 feet. The roar only comes at the time of the charge when he has you where he wants you." ~ Ziden Nutt, Carthage, MO

OFT IN DANGER, OFT IN WOE

Oft in danger, oft in woe,
Onward, Christians, onward go;
Fight the fight, maintain the strife,
Strengthened with the bread of life.

Let your drooping hearts be glad;
March in heavenly armor clad:
Fight, nor think the battle long,
Soon shall victory tune your song.

Onward, then, to glory move,
More than conquerors ye shall prove;
Though opposed by many a foe,
Christian soldiers, onward go.

~ Charles Wesley (1707-1788)

TO GOD BE THE GLORY

To God be the glory, great things he hath done!
So loved he the world that he gave us his Son,
Who yielded his life an atonement for sin,
And opened the lifegate that all may go in.

Refrain:
Praise the Lord, praise the Lord,
Let the earth hear his voice!
Praise the Lord, praise the Lord,
Let the people rejoice!
Come to the Father thru Jesus the Son,
And give him the glory, great things he hath done!

Great things he hath taught us, great things he hath done,
And great our rejoicing thru Jesus the Son;
But purer, and higher, and greater will be
Our wonder, our transport, when Jesus we see.

~ Fanny Crosby (1820-1915)

Bolling Air Force Base, Washington D. C.
Photo by son Bruce Edwards, Bloomfield, IN

GIVE HONOR WHERE HONOR IS DUE

Our son, Bruce, who worked for the Department of Defense at Boling Air Force Base in Maryland, sent the above photo which he explained as follows:

> Navy honor guard casket bearers-in-training are required to carry a weighted casket with them everywhere they go. This photo was taken just outside one of the base dining halls. I guess it must be "Bring Your Casket to Chow" day. Here they set them down so they could go into the building. One of my office mates suggested that I should have climbed into one and waited for them to return.

I have no idea why, but when I looked at the photo it prompted me to sing that old childhood song with new words... *"A tisket, a tasket, a picnic table casket. Carried the casket to the hall and on the way I dropped it..."* I'm assuming the bearers-in-training use a weighted casket for practice so they would be skilled enough NOT to drop one during an actual ceremony.

Being a member of the Casket Bearers Platoon of the United States Navy Ceremonial Guard is not to be taken lightly. Before they are chosen, they are carefully screened. They experience a constant routine of drilling, weight training and grooming more intense than any boot camp. Each body bearing team of six practices many months to develop synchronized motion and ceremonial excellence. It is an expression of respect and honor for deceased servicemen. Not only do they give honor where honor is due, they do it with an expression in their eyes that reflects their feelings of privilege for being a part of it.

It reminds me of the Scripture in Luke 9:23, *"Then (Jesus) said to them all: 'If anyone would come after me, he must deny himself and take up his cross daily and follow me.'"* We are to willingly take up our cross just as He did. A cross is a burden we choose to carry, sometimes for ourselves, but many times for others. To bear that burden, we must develop our spiritual muscles. As we do, our burden becomes lighter, and our facial expression transitions from *"Oh woe is me"* to the same one Moses wore on his face after spending time in God's presence. *"When (Moses) came out...they saw that his face was radiant."* (Exodus 34:34-35)

We are Christian bearers-in-training, and our purpose is to give honor where honor is due! *"Declare (God's) glory among the nations, his marvelous deeds among all peoples. For great is the LORD and most worthy of praise..."* (Psalm 96:3-4)

PONDERINGS

~ Where does our society tend to give honor when it is NOT due?

~ Read 1 Corinthians 10:31. In what ways can we honor God in our everyday activities?

~ Read Galatians 6:2. In what ways can carrying burdens for others strengthen our spiritual muscles?

You are worthy, our Lord and God, to receive glory and honor and power, for you created all things, and by your will they were created and have their being. Amen. (Revelation 4:11)

PSALM 150

Praise the LORD.
Praise God in his sanctuary;
Praise him in his mighty heavens.
Praise him for his acts of power;
Praise him for his surpassing greatness.
Praise him with the sounding of the trumpet,
Praise him with the harp and lyre,
Praise him with tambourine and dancing,
Praise him with the strings and flute,
Praise him with the clash of cymbals,
Praise him with resounding cymbals.
Let everything that has breath praise the LORD.
Praise the LORD.

LISTEN TO WISDOM

Listen with me! I hear someone calling.
My name is being called out.
Someone is trying to get my attention,
Raising her voice to a shout!

She wants me to gain true understanding,
Lay foolish things aside;
She wants me to use sound judgment each day
And in her discerning abide.

It is the voice of Wisdom I hear;
Her voice speaks what is true.
Her instruction is faultless. Her words are just.
She speaks to me and to you!

Wisdom calls out, her voice loud and clear,
Prompting us to obey.
Come! Won't you listen along with me?
She has worthy things to say!

If we fail to listen, we harm ourselves,
For she knows what is best;
Her knowledge is better than the finest gold
And in it, we are blessed.

Blessed is the one who attends to Wisdom,
Daily watching at her door;
For whoever finds Wisdom also finds life
And favor from the Lord!

~ Idella Pearl Edwards

*"Does not wisdom call out?
Does not understanding raise her voice?"
(Proverbs 8:1)*

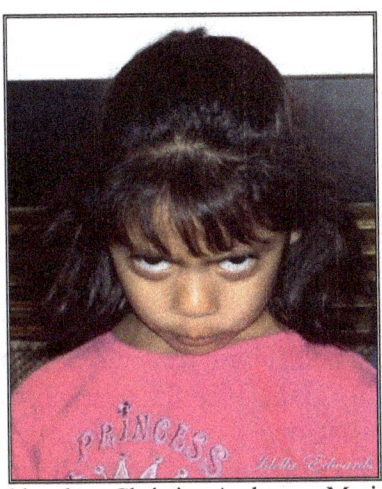

Granddaughter Christine Andersen, Marion, IL

LISTENING

My daughter, Rhonda, shared this story about our granddaughter, Christine, who was 4 years old at the time. Rhonda says: *"I had to discipline Christine this morning for something, so I had her go to her room instead of watching TV while I showered. We still had the baby monitor in her room so I turned it on briefly and happened to catch this little pity-party going on:*

"I don't like this day!" "I don't like Mommy!" "I don't like ANYTHING!" ....pause..........

"I like candy!" "I like TV!" "I like boys!"

Rhonda continues: *"Wait! What did she say? I gave my ears an extra scrubbing."*

If we really listen, we can gather valuable information. I am not a good listener. My family knows they need to get my attention first before they attempt to share anything of significance. I remember one incident years ago. I looked up from the book I was reading and noticed my husband facing the wall, having a one-sided conversation. *"Hello, Wall! How are you today, Wall?"* He was trying to be cute and clever, and at the same time call attention to my lack of listening skills.

As a child, I can still hear my mother's voice ringing in my ears: *"When you get your nose in a comic book, you don't hear one word I say!"* My lack of listening skills does not stop there. Sometimes I neglect to listen to God's voice. Jesus said, *"My sheep listen to my voice."* (John 10:27) In spite of the noisy bleating of a flock of sheep, when the Shepherd calls, they listen. It requires tuning in to the right sound.

Sometimes, in order to tune in, we first need to tune out. I took piano lessons at Olivet Nazarene College in 1958. The minute I walked into Goodwin Hall, I could hear six or seven musical instruments all going at once, in addition to the sound of voice students practicing their vocal scales – all creating an instant meshing of various melodies and tempos to produce the sound of total chaos. Once I arrived at my assigned room, however, and began to practice piano, I was able to tune out the other sounds and hear only my own. Tuning in to God's voice requires tuning out the voices of the world.

In Matthew 17:5, when Jesus was on the mountain with Peter, James and John, *"...a voice from the cloud said, 'This is my Son, whom I love; with him I am well pleased. Listen to him!'"* It's time to listen!

PONDERINGS

~ Was there a specific time you heard God's voice? What were the circumstances? What action did you take?

~ What percentage of our prayer time should be spent in listening?

~ Read 1 Samuel 3:1-10. If we prayed, *"Speak, Lord, for your servant is listening"*....how might our life change?

Oh Great Spirit, whose voice I hear in the winds...let me walk in beauty and make my eyes behold the red and purple sunset. Make my hands respect the things you have made and my ears sharp to hear your voice. Amen.   ~ Lakota Sioux Chief Yellow Lark

My sheep listen to my voice;
I know them, and they follow me.

~ John 10:27

My child, listen to me
and treasure my instructions.
Tune your ears to wisdom,
and concentrate on understanding.

~ Proverbs 2:1-2

Deer photo by Rebecca Odle, Marion, IL
(Rebecca Odle Photography and Designs)

Raccoon photo by Debbie Martin, Dickinson, TX

Photo by Joshua Roman, New York, NY

IN COMMUNITY

In 1977, we moved to Lusby, Maryland and joined a great church. We met with several other church members and decided to plant a community garden on some church-owned land across the road from the church. We worked together to prepare the ground and plant the seeds. Then various members signed up for time slots to water and weed. We anticipated that our faithful joint effort would reward us with a plentiful harvest, but we were in for a surprise.

Our first trip to gather produce was very disappointing. The deer had eaten half the corn, the raccoons ate one bite out of every single watermelon and the tomatoes were gone completely.

One of our church members, a farmer, felt sorry for us and decided to come to our rescue. Every Sunday for the next several weeks, he backed up his pick-up truck beside the church door. It was laden with produce from his garden - melons, cucumbers, tomatoes, potatoes, corn, green beans, etc. Not only did he offer a generous quantity to each member at no cost, he also provided the bags in which to carry it home. We were grateful.

The community garden would have been a wonderful way to have good fellowship, enjoy good food and a great way to save money…had we the foresight to prepare for intruders.

Our spiritual growth is like a community garden. In our endeavor to grow spiritually and please our Heavenly Father, we are in community. We need each other! The Bible explains how we need each other by showing how each body part needs all the other parts. *"As it is, there are many parts, but one body. The eye cannot say to the hand, 'I don't need you!' And the head cannot say to the feet, 'I don't need you!'"* (1 Corinthians 12:20-21)

In our spiritual community garden, there are things that will eat away at our spiritual health and prevent us from reaching our God-given goals. We must have the foresight to prepare for intruders and the willingness to work together to block their access.

In addition to sowing the seeds of God's Kingdom, we must also be willing to fight the good fight together. Sometimes it means storming the gates of Heaven in prayer. Sometimes it means planning ahead and building fences together. Sometimes it means putting on the full armor of God and fighting side by side. We are the body of Christ - in community.

PONDERINGS

~ Why do we often tough it out rather than ask for help?

~ We are relational creatures designed for community. How does sin threaten community?

~ What expressions of love have you experienced as part of God's family?

Lord, as there is but one Body and one Spirit, one hope of our calling, one Lord, one Faith, one Baptism, one God and Father of us all, so we may be all of one heart and of one soul, united in one holy bond of truth and peace, of faith and charity, and may with one mind and one mouth glorify Thee; through Jesus Christ our Lord. Amen. ~ Book of Common Prayer (1928)

AAARGH!

NEVERTHELESS

I once experienced the pain of having the shingles virus. Let me hasten to say, "I do not like pain!" It was not a fun time. Although anti-viral medicines may shorten the duration of the disease, there is no cure. It's a helpless feeling knowing nothing can be done. It's simply a long painful battle of waiting.

NEVERTHELESS, I survived. Life is like that. We must go through some things we do not like. Sometimes, if we are told we will never make it, we give up and stop trying. Other times, if someone predicts our failure, it fuels our determination to prove them wrong and try even harder.

The dictionary definition of the word "NEVERTHELESS" says "*in spite of*" or "*despite anything to the contrary.*" During my battle with shingles, it seemed I would never be pain free again but, to the contrary, my body is now back to normal. My recovery was not the result of my own efforts, but simply a healing process from a loving God. There was nothing I could do. NEVERTHELESS, there are other situations in which God expects us to fight the odds, put forth an extreme effort and go all out for victory.

In the book of 2 Samuel, King David was mocked and told he could not capture the city of Jerusalem:

"You will not get in here; even the blind and the lame can ward

you off." They thought, *"David cannot get in here."* NEVERTHELESS, David captured the fortress of Zion, the City of David. (2 Samuel 5:6-7)

We need to add the word "NEVERTHELESS" to our vocabulary. Satan does everything in his power to make us feel weak and helpless. NEVERTHELESS, we "*can do all things through Christ who strengthens (us)."* (Philippians 4:13 NKJV)

In Nehemiah 4, Sanballat heard that the Jews were rebuilding the wall around Jerusalem. He tried to intimidate them. He ridiculed them saying, *"What are those feeble Jews doing? Will they restore their wall? Will they offer sacrifices? Will they finish in a day? Can they bring the stones back to life from those heaps of rubble - burned as they are?"* Tobiah said, *"What they are building - if even a fox climbed up on it, he would break down their wall of stones!"* (vs. 1-3) NEVERTHELESS, the wall was completed in 52 days.

There are many problems in this world. Yes, we are weak and vulnerable. NEVERTHELESS, with the help of our God, we, too, can overcome!

PONDERINGS

~ Can you think of a recent experience where you fought against the odds and won? What are some things you have overcome?

~ Read Revelation 3:21. What are your biggest fears? Are those fears valid? What can you do to overcome them?

~ What obstacles would you like to overcome this week? Do you need help? From whom?

I'm pressing on the upward way, New heights I'm gaining every day; Still praying as I'm onward bound, "Lord, plant my feet on higher ground." Amen.
~ Lyrics by Johnson Oatman, Jr., (1856-1922)

Tahquamenon Falls, Paradise, Michigan
Oil Painting by Idella Edwards

POSITIVE OVERFLOW

The Body & Soul group at our church held a devotional writing contest. The winner was Sharon Johnson, Marion, Illinois. Her entry is as follows...

"Miriam Webster's definition of 'overflow': *'To fill a space to capacity and spread beyond its limits.'* Overflowing sewers, drains, coffee pots and showers all spell MESS! It's never a good day for an overflow, but the timing of an overflowing toilet was particularly unwelcome and stressful when my husband was just home recovering from surgery. When the standard plunging was no help, I knew I needed a plumber. With visions of dollar signs dancing in my head, I called for help. Hours later and the bank account several hundred dollars lighter, we were back in business. The problem? It seems that roots from nearby trees had grown into the sewer line and blocked the necessary flow from the toilet.

"Jesus taught that the overflow in our lives comes from things stored up in the heart. *'The good man brings good things out of the good stored up in his heart, and the evil man brings evil things out of the evil stored up in his heart. For out of the overflow of his heart his mouth speaks.'* (Luke 6:45)

"Surely, the entire above-mentioned overflow belongs in the evil category, wouldn't you agree? The point I don't want to miss is that Jesus did say also that there is the potential for good overflow as well! One morning as I was doing my devotional reading of the Scripture, the Holy Spirit surprised me by spotlighting two phrases in particular in Colossians 2:6-7: *'So then, just as you received Christ Jesus as Lord, continue to live <u>in him</u>, strengthened in the faith as you were taught, and <u>overflowing with thankfulness</u>'*

"In Luke 6:45, those words, 'in him' and 'overflowing with thankfulness', brought a smile to my face. With the guidance of the Holy Spirit, I was onto something good and began to watch for Scriptures that spoke of overflow resulting from life 'in him'.

"What am I storing up to overflow from my heart today? What is my mouth speaking? Am I overflowing with anger, a judgmental spirit or fear? Many Scriptures give us hope that in Christ we have the potential to overflow with love, joy, comfort, praise and the glory of God.

"I challenge you to start your own search of positive overflow verses and set your heart on storing up all the benefits of life in Christ. May you speak blessings into the lives of those around you as you overflow with the goodness and love of Jesus Christ."

PONDERINGS

~ Would you compare your positive overflow to a waterfall or a drippy faucet?

~ Read Luke 6:38. How has the "law of return" worked in your life? Give an example.

~ Which family member needs you to share your positive overflow this week? Which church member? Which neighbor?

Lord, help me to do nothing out of selfish ambition or vain conceit, but in humility consider others better than myself and look not only to my own interests, but also to the interests of others. Amen.
~ Based on Philippians 2:3-4

Hampton Chapel, Michigamme United Methodist Institute
Photo by son Bruce Edwards, Bloomfield, IN

SOME UNKNOWN REASON

Our son, Bruce, shares the following story:

> When we were two years old, my wife Mary and I both lived in Newberry, Michigan, where her father was our pastor. In 1967, my family moved to Ohio just after my kindergarten year. In 1969, Mary's family attended a Methodist family camp in Michigamme, Michigan. Her father fell in love with the camp and invited us the next year. My family continued attending year after year. When we moved to Maryland, the distance prevented us from going.
>
> In 1981, my family moved to Illinois and planned to attend camp again after an absence of five years, but my boss flatly informed me that his vacation was scheduled then so I could not go. At the last minute, however, he said that for SOME UNKNOWN REASON, circumstances changed his plans so I was free to go. At the same time, Mary was working in Detroit and didn't relish the nine hour drive so had planned to stay home but at the last minute, for SOME UNKNOWN REASON, decided to go.
>
> When I arrived at camp, the first person I saw was Mary, standing by her mother. I secretly elbowed Mom and whispered, *"Mom, is that Mary?"* All the while Mary was elbowing her Mum and whispering, *"Mum, is that Bruce?"* We started dating that week while the whole camp watched and smiled. Mary's dad would

send a young girl named Judy to spy on us and report back to him how we were developing. Grandma Fran would sit on the piano bench with Mary and whisper in her ear, *"You know you've only got a week."* With our heads in the clouds with each other, we didn't notice the whole camp secretly cheering us on.

However, on the way home from camp, I told mom that Mary was just a camp romance, and there was another girl back in Illinois I was interested in. Mom just smiled. The next week, Mary's dad invited me to come for a visit over Labor Day. To this day, no one can remember why I decided to go, but for SOME UNKNOWN REASON, I drove to Iron Mountain and spent the long weekend cementing a relationship with Mary.

We were married August 6, 1983, in the beautiful log chapel at Michigamme. (An interesting side note...my father had knelt at that very same altar at the age of 16 and gave his life to Jesus.) Since our wedding, we continued to take our 2 sons to camp, and also served as dean of the camp for six years. Over the past 40+ years, God has used Family Camp to shower us with special friendships and to bring together one man and one woman who were meant to be together for a lifetime.

We don't see the same big picture that God sees. Jesus told Simon Peter in John 13:7, *"You do not realize now what I am doing, but later you will understand."* For SOME UNKNOWN REASON, God has a plan for each one of us. That plan will bless our lives.

PONDERINGS

~ Read Hebrews 11:6. What part does faith play in discovering the good that God has planned for our lives?

~ Read Proverbs 3:5. Why is it so tempting to lean on our own understanding?

~ How do we know if we are following God's plan?

> God, Who searches the hidden secrets of the heart, satisfy our deep unspoken longings, and enable us by your Spirit to apprehend your purpose. Amen. ~ Acts of Devotion (1927)

Clock Tower, Marion, IL

THE CLOCK IS MOVING

I finally decided to stop dying my hair, revealing my *natural* color (or lack thereof.) I began turning gray at a very young age, and in the beginning, my main reason for using hair dye was so I would not appear to be my husband's mother. Since my husband and I are now "elderly", my original excuse is no longer valid.

When we are young, we can't wait to grow up. I remember one Christmas when I was bitterly disappointed with the gift my father gave me. I was hoping to start a collection of storybook dolls from different countries in fabulous evening gowns. Instead, I received a small cuddly baby doll in a pink blanket. I felt much too grown up for baby dolls, and I was disappointed that he had not noticed.

When we are young, we want the clock to speed up, but after a certain age, we would give anything to slow it down. Age, however, is determined by so much more than an accumulation of years. My mother, who passed away at the age of 100, always seemed so much younger than she actually was. She led an active life...crocheting, playing the piano, square dancing, hunting, fishing and playing games on her own computer. She was always willing to try anything at least once. She took her first airplane ride at the age of 75, and at age 76, went whitewater rafting. When she was 80, she would often walk a mile down the road to a restaurant for Belgian waffles after my husband and I left for work. One time at a Senior Citizens' outing, she was the only Senior willing to take a ride to the top of the trees in a cherry picker.

I can't claim nearly as many experiences as my mother, but I am getting old just the same. They say you can tell you are getting older when...your back goes out more often than you do...when your secrets are safe with your friends because they can't remember them either and...when your children are beginning to look middle-aged!

The Psalmist prayed, *"Show me, O LORD, my life's end and the number of my days; let me know how fleeting is my life."* (Psalm 39:4) Life is short. We need to remember that God not only adds years to our lives, but He also adds life to our years. We are called, by God, to make a difference in our world. We are also called to...*"grow in the grace and knowledge of our Lord and Savior Jesus Christ,"* (2 Peter 3:18) and we only have ONE LIFETIME in which to do it.

The clock is moving!

PONDERINGS

~ What should you be doing now, however old you are, to prepare for old age?

~ How would you live your life differently if you found out you only had one year to live?

~ What lasting impact do you hope your life will have after you are gone?

May all I do today reach far and wide, O Lord. My thoughts, my work, my life: make them blessings for Your kingdom; let them go beyond today, O God. Amen.
~ John Henry Newman (1801-1890)

Photo by son-in-law James Andersen, Marion, IL

HOW FLEETING MY LIFE

The message came through. It was loud and clear.
On March 1st, 2010,
My precious life on earth, as I know it,
Could abruptly have come to an end.

In a near-fatal crash on the highway of life,
God gave me a fresh, new start.
He gave me a multitude of new opportunities
To serve Him with all my heart.

O Lord, my God, You have my attention!
Speak! Your servant is listening;
Let every command fall like sweet dew from heaven
Until my whole world is glistening.

Just like Jonah, may I quickly respond
To throw everything off the boat;
'Til meaningless things sink out of sight,
And only Your Word is afloat.

O Lord, my God, how fleeting my life!
Show me the number of my days,
That I may value each moment in time
And give You all my praise!

~ *Idella Pearl Edwards*

Photo by Allen Gibbs, Chester, IL

COME HOLY SPIRIT, LORD, OUR GOD

Come, Holy Spirit, Lord our God,
And pour Thy gifts of grace abroad;
Thy faithful people fill with blessing,
Love's fire their hearts possessing.

O Lord, Thou by Thy heavenly Light
Dost gather and in faith unite
Through all the world a holy nation
To sing to Thee with exultation,
Hallelujah! Hallelujah!

O holiest Fire! O Source of rest!
Grant that with joy and hope possessed,
And in Thy service kept forever,
Naught us from Thee may sever.

~ Lyrics by Martin Luther (1483-1546)

Photo by son Bruce Edwards, Bloomfield, IN

AS GOOD AS A FIRE

We have all heard the saying, *"Every move is as good as a fire."* I can vouch for that one! I have lived in eight states and twenty-six houses. Moving means transporting great amounts of "stuff" accumulated over the years.

Some of our family's moves were company transfers, so moving expenses were covered. I remember the move from Lusby, Maryland to Downers Grove, Illinois. The company even provided packers. They were very thorough ... maybe a little too thorough. No one in our family has ever smoked, but the packers were smokers. I was able to scrounge up an old dish they could use for an ashtray. When we began unpacking at the other end, I found the dish all wrapped up neatly in white paper - cigarette butts and all.

When we moved from Las Vegas to Oklahoma City we had to cover our own moving expenses because it was a new job, not a job transfer. The moving company charged by the pound, so we decided to pare down as much weight as possible. I donated five large boxes of books to the church library and various friends. My husband moved to Oklahoma City to start work and buy our new home while I stayed behind to sell the old house.

When I finally joined him and walked into our new home, I had a surprise. My husband had purchased a house full of built-in bookshelves. The living room had one entire wall of floor-to-ceiling bookshelves, and the family room had one as well...and I had very few books. I took my time choosing new books, some through garage sales, some through sales at the library and added some to my "Santa" list. I wanted the books on our shelves to represent our family well and do more than just sit on a shelf looking pretty. My goal was to accumulate books that would benefit our family mentally, emotionally and spiritually - books to expand our horizons, books to encourage peace and relaxation and books to challenge our souls to grow.

We all have mental bookshelves full of life's accumulated memories, thoughts and beliefs. Some are beneficial. Some just weigh us down. It may be time to sort and throw. We must selectively restock our mental bookshelves with thoughts and attitudes that represent Christ well. We need a *thought library* that will challenge us to grow mentally, emotionally and spiritually. To do this, we need the help of the Holy Spirit.

In Luke 3:16, John the Baptist tells of the coming of Jesus; *"He will baptize you with the Holy Spirit and with fire."* The baptism of the Holy Spirit is *as good as a fire*. It consumes the old, purifies the new and gives us a *thought library* we can be proud of.

PONDERINGS

~ Do you tend to be a saver or a tosser? Why?

~ What thoughts and attitudes do we need to toss from our mental library? Would a fire help? How do we light our spiritual fire?

~ Read Romans 12:2. How do we "renew our mind" and how often should it be done?

May the light of God illumine the heart of my soul. May the flame of Christ kindle me to love. May the fire of the Spirit free me to live this day, tonight, and forever. Amen   ~ Celtic Benediction

Photo by granddaughter Courtney Edwards, Murphysboro, IL

SEND THE FIRE!

Thou Christ of burning, cleansing flame,
Send the fire, send the fire!
Thy blood-bought gift today we claim,
Send the fire, send the fire!

For strength to ever do the right,
For grace to conquer in the fight,
For power to walk the world in white,
Send the fire, send the fire!

To make our weak hearts strong and brave,
Send the fire, send the fire!
To live a dying world to save,
Send the fire, send the fire!

~ William Booth (1829-1912)
Founder of the Salvation Army

THE SUNFLOWER SURPRISE

There they were on the dining room table,
Displayed in a clear, blue vase.
I stopped and stared, my eyes full of wonder
As a look of delight found my face.

Giant sunflowers, bright red and yellow,
Dyed to look like fire,
Wearing the sunlight that streamed in the window
Like joyful, festive attire.

A gift from my hubby, for no other reason
Than to add a sparkle to my eyes;
A gift for his wife, the love of his life,
A sweet and lovely surprise.

My heart did a dance with an upward glance,
Praising the Good Lord above,
For giving to me this wonderful man
To have and to hold and to love.

~ Idella Pearl Edwards

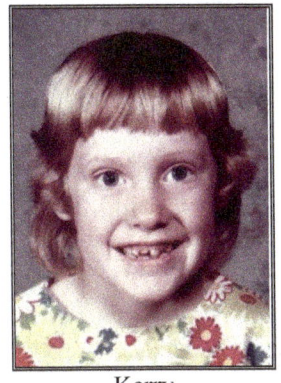

Kerry   A Tooth Fairy (a.k.a. Sarah Martin, Yukon, OK)

TAKEN BY SURPRISE

We enjoyed the four years we spent living in Tornado, West Virginia. Our youngest daughter, Kerry, was in grade school at the time and shares this memory.

> I spent part of my childhood in West Virginia and absolutely loved it there. I used to play with the puff mushrooms in the natural sandbox at the entrance to the forest, hunt for jewel weeds, wander in the wild wheat field, climb the mountain sides in the summer and sled them in the winter, catch blue gill in summer and skate the pond in the winter and of course, shoot the rapids in the river.
>
> Oh! And, of course, there was the candy store within walking distance where they actually let us go BEHIND the counter! And Easter Morning Sunrise Service on the top of the mountain, watching the sunrise create a silhouette from the cross, was a wonderful experience. Yup. I loved it there!

Living in West Virginia was like stepping back in time. Many community activities revolved around the fire station or the church. There was a corner lot where everyone gathered on Friday nights in the summer to play volleyball. For our annual Easter Sunday Sunrise Service, we met at the base of the hill and, using flashlights, we climbed the mountain in the dark to await the sunrise at the top.

One time, on the way up, Kerry managed to wiggle free a loose tooth. She told me about it and then put the tooth in her jacket pocket. She was completely taken by surprise later when she discovered the tooth missing and a quarter in its place. (A visit from the Tooth Fairy is always a magical moment.) As we waited for the sunrise, she held the quarter tightly in her little hand.

The very first Easter held some surprises as well. In John, Chapter 20, Mary Magdalene went to the tomb and was surprised to find the 2000-pound stone rolled away and two angels inside the tomb. She was also surprised when she thought she was talking to the gardener but discovered it was Jesus. She was filled with joy.

It should come as no great surprise to us that Jesus is walking beside us, even when we are unaware of His presence. Just as Mary was downcast with the death of her Lord, we are so absorbed with the grief of our problems that we miss the joy of God's presence. God told Joshua "...*I will be with you; I will never leave you nor forsake you,*" (Joshua 1:5) and Jesus told his disciples, "*...I am with you always, to the very end of the age.*" (Matthew 28:20) We should never be *taken by surprise* when God decides to bless us!

PONDERINGS

~ Have you ever felt alone, abandoned by God? When?

~ Read Zephaniah 3:17. Does it surprise you that, in spite of all your failures, God takes great delight in you? How do we wrap our minds around that kind of love?

~ What are some ways that God expects us to surprise others with joy this week?

Joyful, joyful, we adore Thee, God of glory, Lord of love;
Hearts unfold like flowers before Thee, opening to the sun above.
Melt the clouds of sin and sadness; drive the dark of doubt away;
Giver of immortal gladness, fill us with the light of day! Amen.
~ Lyrics by Henry J. van Dyke (1852-1933)

PRONE TO WANDER

When I was growing up in Aurora, Illinois in the 50's, an abundance of hobos rode the rails. We lived at the edge of town near a railroad track; therefore, it was not uncommon to have a hobo come to our back door and ask for food. My mother usually fixed scrambled eggs, beans and toast for him. He would sit on the back porch and eat, give us a hearty "thank you" and be on his way.

Since the life of a hobo was a dangerous one, they usually banded together for protection. They also had private symbols they would post on utility poles with charcoal to communicate information to their fellow travelers. Some of the basic messages meant, "doctor, no charge," "you may sleep in barn," "police here frown on hobos," "dangerous neighborhood," or "these people are rich."

Some became hobos because of circumstances, but others were hobos by choice because they were running from responsibility. Neither kind ever bothered to travel with a compass. There was no ultimate direction nor end purpose. Their only goal was to survive one day at a time. Hobos were looked down upon because they made no significant contribution to society.

There is, however, a little hobo in each of us. One of the stanzas in the hymn, "Come Thou Fount Of Every Blessing," (Robert Robinson - 1757) reads:

> May Thy goodness like a fetter,
> Bind my wandering heart to Thee.
> Prone to wander, Lord, I feel it,
> Prone to leave the God I love,
> Here's my heart, O take and seal it,
> Seal it for Thy courts above.

We are all prone to wander. Perhaps not in the same way a hobo wanders, but our hearts can wander from the truth, tempting us to ride the rails of disobedience. We may never jump into a boxcar and flee, but we may go a couple steps in the wrong direction. Our deviation from God's plan is always just one step at a time.

The first line of the stanza asks that God's goodness bind our wandering heart to Him. How can God's goodness police our wanderings? It's simple. The more He reveals His love and compassion to our sinful generation, the more it stirs our grateful hearts and our desire to please Him. The more we are aware of His goodness and mercy, the more our longing soul is satisfied and no longer *prone to wander.*

PONDERINGS

~ What are the characteristics of the person who is prone to wander?

~ Is wandering deliberate, careless or simply the lack of a goal?

~ Read James 5:19-20. What is our responsibility if we see a Christian brother or sister wandering away from the fold?

> O Lord, whose way is perfect, help us, I pray Thee, always to trust in your goodness: that walking with Thee and following Thee in all simplicity, we may possess quiet and contented minds; and may cast all our care on Thee. Amen. ~ Christina Rossetti (1830-1894)

Grandson Jake Murphy, Gyeongsang-do, South Korea

GOOD NEWS

Our grandson, Jacob Murphy, has been on many mission trips. One summer, on his way to Italy, the mission team stopped in Spain. He said, *"I had a great time in Spain. We did some street evangelism, which was a stretch for me, but it was a good experience. I stood on a red box in the middle of Madrid and gave my testimony, having it translated into Spanish. It was a thriller."*

Once they arrived in Italy, the team immediately plunged into the task for which they had been called. Jake shares the following: *"This week has just been crazy with all four of us guys getting here and diving into the preparations for Vacation Bible School. It has been a lot of work but it's been super fun to paint the scenes and start putting together different activities for the children. The kids here in Italy are just amazing, full of so much joy and hope. They are starving for attention and love though, so it is great to be the one who is able to give it to them! It's been an amazing experience, and I have loved getting to see the different things God is doing here in Italy."* Jake and the team were able to share the "good news" with the children of Italy - the good news that there are people who care, but most of all, that there is a God who cares and loves them.

Christ commanded his disciples. *"Go into all the world and preach the good news to all creation."* (Mark 16:15) Are our lips sealed? God has no mouths but ours. This world is filled with bad news. The Bible tells us that the bad news will become worse and worse. 2 Timothy 3:2-4 says, *"People will be lovers of themselves, lovers of money, boastful, proud, abusive, disobedient to their parents, ungrateful, unholy, without love, unforgiving, slanderous, without self-control, brutal, not lovers of the good, treacherous, rash, conceited, lovers of pleasure rather than lovers of God."* If there was ever a time people need to hear good news, it's now! They must be told the good news that God loves them and He's still in the miracle business.

In the 7th Chapter of 2 Kings, during a famine, four lepers stumbled upon an enemy camp and found it empty. They were overjoyed and began to plunder the camp, hiding their treasures. But then they remembered their fellow citizens were also starving. *"...they said to each other, 'We're not doing right. This is a day of good news and we are keeping it to ourselves...'"* (vs. 9)

Yes, people desperately need to hear the *Good News*. And as Jake said, *"It is great to be the one who is able to give it to them!"*

PONDERINGS

~ Why is it important to tell other people about Jesus?

~ What are some challenges you have encountered while sharing the Good News? What victories have you experienced?

~ What are some ways we can share the Good News by our actions?

Everliving God, whose will it is that all should come to you through your Son Jesus Christ: Inspire our witness to him, that all may know the power of his forgiveness and the hope of his resurrection; who lives and reigns with you and the Holy Spirit, one God, now and for ever. Amen.
~ Book of Common Prayer (1928)

Uganda   "JAKE"   Cambodia

Moldova    Romania

India

Ismenius Tiger Butterfly
Photo by Rebecca Odle Photography and Designs

THE BUTTERFLY

I stood by my kitchen window,
Heart heavy with despair.
Hope was gone, my spirit spent,
Unsure that God was there.

My unseeing eyes gazed outward
While inward thoughts ran wild.
Chasing elusive answers,
My soul, by doubt, beguiled.

My mind came into focus
As a movement caught my eye.
Outside among the flowers
Was a colorful butterfly.

It was a vision of beauty,
Dancing in the breeze.
Darting among the flowers,
It fluttered by with ease.

Entranced by this tiny miracle,
Suddenly I knew!
God in all His mercy
Would gently guide me through!

The God who made the universe,
The God who created me,
The God who made the butterfly
Set my spirit free!

~ *Idella Pearl Edwards*

Zebra Butterfly, Costa Rica
Photo by cousin William E. Van Atte, Batchawana Bay, ON

PURSUIT OF HAPPINESS

Sometimes happiness can be as elusive as a butterfly. Virtually everyone wants to be happy. We go to great lengths to pursue happiness by going and doing and buying. These methods, however, do not guarantee happiness. When parents are asked what they want for their child, the usual answer is that they want them to be happy, and yet as we look around our world, we see many people who are discouraged and depressed and looking in the wrong direction for answers. The more we search for happiness through self-indulgence, the more unfulfilled we become.

Nathaniel Hawthorne (1804-1864) once said, *"Happiness is a butterfly, which when pursued, is always just beyond your grasp, but which, if you will sit down quietly, may alight upon you."* There are no easy answers on how to find happiness, but those who pursue it full force by attempting to gratify the desires of the flesh will find it more elusive than the butterfly. Happiness, in fact, seems to be a by-product of selfless living. Isaiah 58:9-10 tells us, *"...If you do away with the yoke of oppression, with the pointing finger and malicious talk, and if you spend yourselves in behalf of the hungry and satisfy the needs of the oppressed, then your light will rise in the darkness, and your night will become like the noonday."*

One of our friends from Maryland, Ginger Hopwood, shares the following story:

> There are STILL GOOD PEOPLE in this world. This just happened: I'm in Wally World getting the oil changed, and a man comes in wanting to know if anyone reported money missing. Right as he starts to leave, the phone at the counter rings, and a person calls to say he lost some money. The man is now waiting for the person to come get it. Now that was a God ordained moment. The gentleman who found the money has integrity and good morals. May God bless your honesty! By the way, the amount was $250.00.

My guess is that the person who lost the money was extremely happy to get it back. However, the one who returned the money will be rewarded with an internal joy that will bring a deep peace to his soul.

You've heard the expression, *"You can't outgive God!"* 2 Corinthians 9:6 tells us, *"Remember this: Whoever sows sparingly will also reap sparingly, and whoever sows generously will also reap generously."* This verse is a great one to remember in our pursuit of happiness!

PONDERINGS

~ Complete this sentence: *"I would be happy if only...."*

~ Read John 15:9-12. Jesus' words about joy are sandwiched between words about love? What does this tell us?

~ What are some ways we can make other people happy?

Lord, You have made known to me the path of life; you will fill me with joy in your presence, with eternal pleasures at your right hand. Amen. (Psalm 16:11)

Photo by Laura Lovell, Oklahoma City, OK

"The butterfly is a flying flower; the flower is a tethered butterfly."
~ *Ponce Denis Écouchard Lebrun (1729-1807)*

Photos by Brian R. Jennings, Pittsburgh, PA

85

"Lenny Boris"
Photo by Liz Reynolds, Marion, IL

Open my eyes that I may see
Glimpses of truth thou hast for me;
Place in my hands the wonderful key
That shall unclasp and set me free.

Silently now I wait for thee,
Ready, my God, thy will to see.
Open my eyes, illumine me,
Spirit divine!

~ Lyrics by Clara H. Scott, (1841-1897)

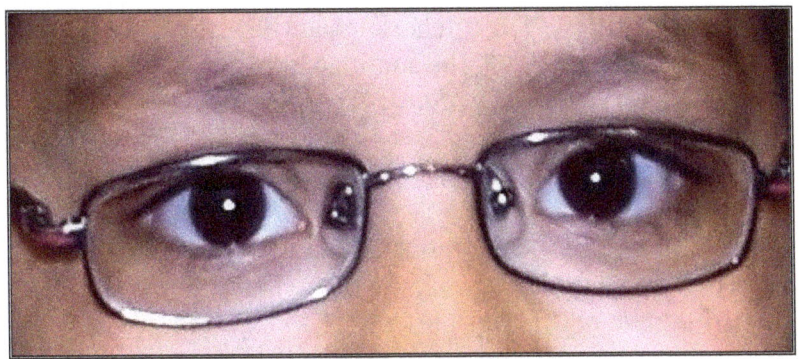

Grandson David Andersen, Marion, IL

WATCH WHERE YOU'RE GOING!

We don't always look where we are going. Our daughter and family live close by. When our grandson, David, was about eight years old, he would ride his bike (1/2 mile) to our house with dad and little sister. David always arrived a good five minutes before Daddy and Christine.

One particular day, David rushed into the house all excited because he had won a game on his hand-held computer. It seems he was trying to win the game with one hand, all the while riding as fast as he could to win the bicycle race with Daddy and Christine.

Many of us are into multi-tasking, but there are some things that merit our full attention and could get us into trouble by a lack thereof. We need to watch where we're going. Especially spiritually! Psalm 123:1-2 tells us: "*I lift up my eyes to you, to you whose throne is in heaven. As the eyes of slaves look to the hand of their master, as the eyes of a maid look to the hand of her mistress, so our eyes look to the LORD our God, till he shows us his mercy.*"

The eyes of our soul must focus on God! Because He is omnipotent (all-powerful), omnipresent (present everywhere at the same time) and omniscient (all-knowing), He is the best One to follow.

In 2 Chronicles 20:12, King Jehoshaphat knew that his army was no match for the enemy. He admitted to God, "...*we have no power to face this vast army that is attacking us. We do not know what to do, but our eyes are upon you.*" I love the commentary on this verse by Matthew Henry (1662-1714). He says:

> We rely upon thee, and from thee is all our expectation. The disease seems desperate: we know not what to do, are quite at a loss, in a great strait. But this is a sovereign remedy, our eyes are upon thee, an eye of acknowledgment and humble submission, an eye of faith and entire dependence, an eye of desire and hearty prayer, an eye of hope and patient expectation. In thee, O God! do we put our trust; our souls wait on thee.

The question remains…why do we look to this world for answers instead of to the sovereign remedy? If we watch where we are going, we can follow the One Who sees all!

PONDERINGS

~ Are you good at multi-tasking? When is multi-tasking essential, and when could it lead to trouble?

~ Read Psalm 121. Where do YOU look for help?

~ Read Ephesians 6:18. According to this verse, an important area in which to be alert or watchful is our prayer life. Why is this important?

O my Savior, help me.
I am so slow to learn, so prone to forget, so weak to climb;
I am in the foothills when I should be on the heights;
I am pained by my graceless heart, my prayerless days,
I am blind while light shines around me:
Take the scales from my eyes . . .
Make it my chief joy to study thee, meditate on thee, gaze on thee,
And sit like Mary at your feet. Amen.   ~ Old Puritan prayer

Antigua, Guatemala - Agua Volcano
Photo by Kim Vanderhelm, Allendale, MI

PSALM 121

I lift up my eyes to the hills -
Where does my help come from?
My help comes from the LORD,
The Maker of heaven and earth.
He will not let your foot slip -
He who watches over you will not slumber;
Indeed, he who watches over Israel
Will neither slumber nor sleep.

The LORD watches over you -
The LORD is your shade at your right hand;
The sun will not harm you by day,
Nor the moon by night.
The LORD will keep you from all harm -
He will watch over your life;
The LORD will watch over your coming and going
Both now and forevermore.

Lusby, Maryland
Photo by son Bruce Edwards, Bloomfield, IN

WE MUST GET HOME

We must get home! How could we stray like this?--
So far from home, we know not where it is,--
Only in some fair, apple-blossomy place
Of children's faces--and the mother's face--
We dimly dream it, till the vision clears
Even in the eyes of fancy, glad with tears.

We must get home--for we have been away
So long, it seems forever and a day!
And O so very homesick we have grown,
The laughter of the world is like a moan
In our tired hearing, and its song as vain,--
We must get home--we must get home again!

We must get home again--we must--we must!--
(Our rainy faces pelted in the dust)
Creep back from the vain quest through endless strife
To find not anywhere in all of life
A happier happiness than blest us then ...
We must get home--we must get home again!

~ James Whitcomb Riley (1849-1916)

Lusby, Maryland (my favorite home!)
Photo by son Bruce Edwards, Bloomfield, IN

THERE'S NO PLACE LIKE HOME!

There are times when home doesn't feel like home. We have lived in eight states. Each time my husband and I moved to another state, we would try to make the new house seem like home as quickly as possible. Before all the boxes were unpacked, we would stop and hang pictures on the walls. Seeing the familiar paintings and photographs when we walked through the house seemed to be very comforting.

We also enjoy the comfort of home after we have been away for a while. Going on vacation is great - seeing new sights, tasting new foods and having new adventures. There comes a time, however, when we just want to go home. We want to do normal things, see old friends and sleep in our own beds.

One time, I was in the hospital for surgery, came home and then went back by ambulance a few days later with an obstruction. Although the hospital staff was friendly and compassionate, it was not like home. If there were a few restful moments, they were interrupted by staff taking blood, taking vitals or just checking to see if I needed anything. My comfort level was at its lowest point with the pain of surgery, being tethered to an IV pole and having a large plastic tube running down my nose into my stomach. Needless to say, I just wanted to go home!

After being held captive for 70 years in Babylon, the Israelites had lost all hope of ever returning to their beloved home. When they were finally allowed to go home, their joy was overwhelming: *"When the LORD brought back the captives to Zion, we were like men who dreamed. Our mouths were filled with laughter, our tongues with songs of joy..."* (Psalm 126:1-2)

We tend to take our homes for granted. Peggy Maragni (Marion, Illinois), who helps feed the homeless at a mission called The Promise, said:

> I have taken a lot of people home, but when you take a homeless person home it's a little different. Drove him to the park and let him out. He waved and said, "I'll see you tomorrow" and "What's for breakfast?" LOL. I love what we do at The Promise. We fall in love with everyone who comes through our door.

I'm sure The Promise felt more like home to him than his park bench. Home should be a place where we are loved and accepted, and where we are intimately acquainted with others. Someday, we will have the ultimate home. Jesus said, *"In my Father's house are many rooms...I am going there to prepare a place for you...I will come back and take you to be with me that you also may be where I am."* (John 14:2-3) There's no place like home!

PONDERINGS

~ Did you ever run away from home? Explain.

~ What are some things that make your house feel like home?

~ Read Deuteronomy 6:6-9. What does this verse tell us about God's expectations of the home.

How lovely is your dwelling place, O LORD Almighty! My soul yearns, even faints, for the courts of the LORD; my heart and my flesh cry out for the living God. Amen.   (Psalm 84:1,2,4)

HOME! SWEET HOME!

Mid pleasures and palaces though we may roam,
Be it ever so humble, there's no place like home;
A charm from the sky seems to hallow us there,
Which, seek through the world, is ne'er met with elsewhere.

Home, home, sweet, sweet home!
There's no place like home,
Oh, there's no place like home!

To thee I'll return, overburdened with care;
The heart's dearest solace will smile on me there;
No more from that cottage again will I roam;
Be it ever so humble, there's no place like home.

~ Lyrics by John Howard Payne (1791-1852)

Last night at Bible study, a mother brought her son and daughter, and after the study I gave the little girl a couple of dolls, and she said. "NOW THEY WILL HAVE A REAL HOME!" I thought to myself that some of these kids don't know what a real home is. I'm so glad for The Promise where people come and sit and say. "This place feels like home!" Let's never take it for granted what God has blessed us with. A HOME!   ~ Peggy Maragni, THE PROMISE, Marion, IL.

Desert Willow (Orchid of the Desert), Phoenix, AZ
Photo by Janet Hatfield, Middletown, IN

GOD'S WORLD OF FLOWERS

Have you ever looked closely at the beauty of an iris,
Or studied the center of a rose?
With colors so vibrant and soft and deep,
Each flower literally glows.

Have you ever buried your face in a lilac,
Deeply inhaling its treasure?
A haunting fragrance so enchantingly sweet,
It fills the soul with pleasure.

How long since you gazed at a bright, yellow daisy,
Or studied a pansy's sweet face?
How long since you truly admired an orchid,
A flower of beauty and grace.

God's world of flowers awaits you, my friend,
Worthy of admiration.
There is beauty to behold and velvet to touch
In every pink carnation.

~ Idella Pearl Edwards

Genny Chaussé
Photo by Melissa Chaussé, Marion, IL

TAKE TIME TO SMELL THE FLOWERS

We are a nation in a hurry. You've heard the prayer: *"Lord, give me patience, and I want it right now."* We are afflicted with *hurry-itis*. We don't like waiting in traffic, in the doctor's office or when our computers don't work fast enough. There are multiple Scripture verses that tell us to wait on the Lord. Psalm 27:14 says, *"Wait for the LORD; be strong and take heart and wait for the LORD."* And while we are waiting, we might as well take time to smell the flowers.

Francis de Sales (1567-1622) said, *"Never be in a hurry; do everything quietly and in a calm spirit. Do not lose your inner peace for anything whatsoever, even if your whole world seems upset."*

My husband is a Type A personality with little patience for waiting. When he went on a mission trip to Mexico, however, he had to adjust to their laid-back, unhurried way of life. Every afternoon, in the heat of the day, they take siestas. The church services are not rushed either; each one lasting a good two hours. The Mexican people are not in a hurry to get things done, but instead, put the emphasis on living in the moment. They tend to have a more relaxed and casual lifestyle, and relationships always come before schedules. The Message Bible says it this way, "*Slow down. Take a deep breath. What's the hurry? Why wear yourself out? Just what are you after anyway?...*" (Jeremiah 2:25)

Many times we miss the roses because we are traveling down the wrong pathway or going through the wrong gate. Matthew 7:13-14 says: *"Enter through the narrow gate. For wide is the gate and broad is the road that leads to destruction, and many enter through it. But small is the gate and narrow the road that leads to life, and only a few find it."* Going through the wide gate would be much easier and faster. But as Robert Frost said in "The Road Not Taken", *"I took the one less traveled by, and that has made all the difference."*

It will make all the difference in our lives as well when we are willing to slow down and make God's will for our lives a priority. A problem arises when we are in a hurry and God isn't. We can't understand why He doesn't answer our prayer RIGHT NOW! But God doesn't give us His timetable for our lives. Why? Because He wants us to trust Him! In the meantime, He wants us to *take time to smell the flowers*, to enjoy each and every blessing He gives us...all the things that are right beneath our noses.

PONDERINGS

~ Do you tend to drive over the speed limit? Is there a speed limit to life? When does faster become too fast?

~ Read Luke 10:38-42. Which sister was in the biggest hurry? How can we ignore pressing needs to savor the essential?

~ Which blessings might we miss if we rush through life?

O God, Who sends peace to those that receive it; open to us this day the sea of Your love, and water us with the plenteous streams from the riches of Your grace. Make us children of quietness, and heirs of peace. Amen.   ~ Syrian Clementine Liturgy

Nancy McShannon's Tiger Lily, Marion, IL

Judy Arnold's Echinacea, Marion, IL

Where flowers bloom so does hope.

- Lady Bird Johnson (1912-2007)

Nancy McShannon's Honeysuckle, Marion, IL

ALLEGORIES OF FORGIVENESS
The taste, smell, sound, look and feel of God's mercy.

God's forgiveness...

~ Tastes like a hot cup of cocoa on a cold wintry day...

When sin would chill us to the bone,
God kindles a fire within;
He warms us from the inside out
And vaporizes sin.

~ Smells like rain-sweetened air after a spring shower...

When repentance brings us to our knees,
Our sins are washed away;
Refreshed, renewed, we rise in hope
To start a brand new day.

~ Sounds like a joyful melody...

God's mercy gives abundant joy,
More than our hearts can contain;
A song bubbles up from the depths of our soul
As we gratefully praise His Name!

~ Looks like a bridge of reconciliation...

Once we are reconciled to God,
It sets us free to forgive,
To love our neighbors as ourselves,
And teach them how to live.

~ Feels like wind beneath our wings...

God sets us free from the weight of sin
And lifts our eyes on high;
He breaks the hold of the quicksand of doubt
And gives us wings to fly.

~ Idella Pearl Edwards

"Pepsi," Marion, IL

I'M SORRY

How easy is it to say, "I'm sorry"? Our daughter and son-in-law, Rhonda and Jim, have 6 cats. Christine (at the age of eight) wrote a letter to their cat, Pepsi. Rhonda shares the following story:

> Our cat, Pepsi, eats everything. A couple years ago, he ended up with a bowel obstruction and had a costly surgery. Christine is under strict orders to keep her hairbands put away, because Pepsi will find one even in the darkest corner! I confiscated one from him last night. Instead of making Christine write sentences yet again, I told her to write a letter of apology to Pepsi. Here is her letter exactly as written:

"Dear Pepsi, I'm sorry that I let you have that hairband. I really don't want you to die! Plus I want you around because I want someone around thats diffrent! I have tons of memerays to remember! Please help me! Also Pepsi I kown you also love Toby, and Diamond and I kown they love you too! I love you so much and please let me known some how that you love me too! I also like you because when Zoey throws up you are my vacum. My heart would be broken if you died. I kown that Toby's and Diamod's heart would be broken too! Plus your alwasy good at scarying people! Love Christine"

Christine did a good job of apologizing to her cat. Much better than we usually do when we are at fault. Jeremiah 8:4-6 (MSG) says it plainly:

> Tell them this, God's Message: *"Do people fall down and not get up? Or take the wrong road and then just keep going? So why do these people go backwards, and just keep on going - backwards! They stubbornly hold onto their illusions, refuse to change direction. I listened carefully but heard not so much as a whisper. No one expressed one word of regret. Not a single 'I'm sorry' did I hear. They just kept at it, blindly and stupidly banging their heads against a brick wall."*

How many times, even when we find ourselves on the wrong road, do we stubbornly and blindly choose to keep going in the wrong direction? God is waiting to hear a genuine apology. He is waiting for us to stop and change directions. He is waiting to wrap us in arms of love and forgiveness. The Bible tells us that all of heaven rejoices when we humbly kneel and say *"I'm sorry!"*

"I tell you, there will be more joy in heaven over one sinner who repents than over ninety-nine righteous persons who need no repentance." (Luke 15:7)

PONDERINGS

~ Do you have a hard time saying, "I'm sorry"? What fears accompany having to apologize?

~ Is it harder for you to forgive others or yourself? Why?

~ When was the last time you apologized to God?

Dear Lord and Father of mankind, forgive our foolish ways! Reclothe us in our rightful mind, in purer lives Thy service find, in deeper reverence, praise. Amen.
~ Lyrics by John Greenleaf Whittier (1807-1892)

Oral Roberts University, Tulsa, OK

THE LITTLE BENCH

There's a little bench at the front of the church
Where you can go and kneel
And bring all your troubles and heartaches
And give them to Jesus to heal

Don't worry if words won't come
Lay your head on Jesus' breast and cry
He knows your heart and understands your tears
And He will wipe them dry

Jesus bought us with His life
And He always takes care of His own
But some of His children are determined
To carry their burdens back home

How sad to see God's troubled child
Sitting so perfectly still
When there's a little bench at the front of the church
Where he can go and kneel.

~ Sharon Hubbell
Marion, Illinois

First Landing Cross, Virginia Beach, VA
(The first place the pilgrims landed in 1607)
Photo by Danielle Barter, Marion, IL

THE CROSS

Through the years
The cross stands tall,
An emblem of
God's love for all.
What more could God
Have ever done,
Than sacrifice
His only Son?

Jesus took
My sin and shame;
Took upon
Himself the blame.
I thank my God
On bended knee
That Jesus paid
The debt for me.

~ Idella Pearl Edwards

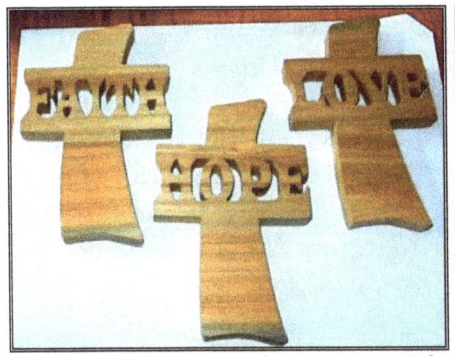

Photos by son Bruce Edwards, Bloomfield, IN

THE GREATEST OF THESE IS LOVE

Our son, Bruce, enjoys making things with his scroll saw. When he lived in Maryland, his pastor at New Life Wesleyan Church (La Plata, Maryland) gave him an old rotting bench which Bruce redesigned and rebuilt for him. He made crosses and cut out the words, "faith", "hope" and "love" and set them in the back of the bench. His pastor was very pleased when he received it.

Bruce shares the following:
> Pastor Chris Wagnon shared a great story at church last night about their new bench and their 3-year-old granddaughter. He said his granddaughter led him to the bench and said, *"Papa, you sit on Love and I'll sit on Hope."* So they sat, Papa's granddaughter snuggling up next to him on the bench.
>
> A minute later, the granddaughter said, *"I'm going to sit on Love now."* When Chris started to get up, she said, *"No Papa, stay there."* As he sat back down, she quickly climbed onto his lap.

1 Corinthians 13:13 tells us: *"Now these three remain: faith, hope and love. But the greatest of these is love."* Although faith and hope are important, the Scripture tells us love is the greatest. How great is love? It would be difficult to imagine what our world would be like without it. 1st Corinthians 13 tells us that without love, we are nothing. It explains the greatness of love by listing all its marvelous characteristics, detailing what love IS and what it is NOT; what it ALWAYS does and what it NEVER does. God

Himself is our example. He exemplifies each and every quality. In fact the Bible tells us that God IS love. (1 John 4:16)

Is it possible for us to love like God loves? Oswald Chambers, in his book, "My Utmost For His Highest," said, *"The Holy Spirit reveals to me that God loved me not because I am lovable, but because it was His nature to do so. Now He commands me to show the same love to others by saying, '...love one another as I have loved you.'"* (John 15:12)

Although love is an emotion, it is also a choice. Jesus asks us to choose love, not only when it is emotionally easy, but even when it is extremely difficult to do so. He even asks us to love our enemies. (Matthew 5:44) It is not our human nature to love those who seem unlovable, but God never commands us to do anything that He does not give us the strength and power to accomplish. *"...with God all things are possible."* (Matthew 19:26)

Yes, love is a choice. It's not only a good choice, but it's a God choice because God proclaimed it to be the GREATEST.

PONDERINGS

~ Do you love yourself? What often keeps a person from loving himself? How does this affect his love for others?

~ Read 1 John 3:17-18. How do love and service go hand in hand?

~ Read Luke 10:27. We all fall short of this command. What are some things we can do to increase our love for God?

My Jesus, I love Thee, I know Thou art mine;
For Thee all the follies of sin I resign;
My gracious Redeemer, my Savior art Thou;
If ever I loved Thee, my Jesus, 'tis now. Amen
~ Lyrics by William Ralph Featherston (1848–1875)

THE LOVE OF GOD

The love of God is greater far
Than tongue or pen can ever tell;
It goes beyond the highest star,
And reaches to the lowest hell;
The guilty pair, bowed down with care,
God gave His Son to win;
His erring child He reconciled,
And pardoned from his sin.

Oh, love of God, how rich and pure!
How measureless and strong!
It shall forevermore endure,
The saints' and angels' song.

Could we with ink the ocean fill,
And were the skies of parchment made,
Were every stalk on earth a quill,
And every man a scribe by trade;
To write the love of God above
Would drain the ocean dry;
Nor could the scroll contain the whole,
Though stretched from sky to sky.

~ Frederick M. Lehman (1868-1953)

What an enormous magnifier is tradition!
How a thing grows in the human memory
and in the human imagination,
when love, worship, and all
that lies in the human heart,
is there to encourage it.

~ Thomas Carlyle (1795-1881)

Oil painting by Idella Edwards

TRADITION!

My favorite stage production is "Fiddler On The Roof." During the song, "Tradition", Tevye makes three statements: *"Because of our traditions:* 1) *We've kept our balance for many years.* 2) *Every one of us knows who he is and what God expects him to do.* 3) *Without them, our lives would be as shaky as a fiddler on the roof."*

I recently asked friends to share meaningful traditions their families uphold. Here are a few responses:

Brenda Prell: (Christmas) On Christmas Eve we mix a bowl of reindeer food, consisting of rolled oats and glitter (to help the reindeer find the food) and sprinkle it on the lawn before bedtime.

Cande Nicks: (Thanksgiving) On Thanksgiving, we take time to call family members that we have not heard from in a while and take turns talking to them. We also express what we are thankful for.

Amanda Benson: (Christmas) Love the family going together for the Christmas service at The Chapel with my Grandma. We filled three rows one year.

Virginia Tucker: (Sundays) Every Sunday after church, we drove 26 miles to eat lunch with my Grandparents. I don't remember my parents missing any Sundays.

Jennifer Trusty: (Easter) We are Orthodox Christians. Holding candles at midnight, we sing as we parade outside around the church and when we re-enter the church, it is bathed in light. Bells are ringing! The choir is singing! The people proclaim *"Christ is risen!"* in a myriad of languages: *"Christos Anesti!"* (Greek), *"Kristos Voskrese!"* (Russian), *"Cristo Ha Resucitado!"* (Spanish), and *"Al-Masih-Qam!"* (Arabic), etc. The sermon is the same one given around 400 A.D. by St. John Chrysostom. Hearing these words that have been repeated to millions of people for hundreds of years gives me goose bumps.

In "Fiddler On The Roof," Tevye fights to keep his traditions and even though he must leave town, he motions the fiddler to come with him, symbolizing that his traditions will always be with him. We, too, should strive to hold on to our traditions. One tradition that should *always* be passed on to future generations is the commands of Jesus to *"Love the Lord your God with all your heart and with all your soul and with all your strength and with all your mind"*; and, *"Love your neighbor as yourself."* (Luke 10:27)

PONDERINGS

~ What is your favorite tradition? Why are traditions comforting?

~ Read Deuteronomy 4:9. How do traditions help us remember? Which traditions would best perpetuate God's truth to future generations?

~ Read Matthew 15:8-9. How would you define an *empty tradition?* What danger signals should we watch for?

Lord, help us to stand fast and hold on to the traditions we were taught; watch ourselves closely that we do not forget the things our eyes have seen so that future generations may come to know You. Amen.   (Based on 2 Thessalonians 2:15 & Deuteronomy 4:9)

I have hidden your word in my heart that I might not sin against you. ~ Psalm 119:11

A GOOD TRADITION

Love the LORD your God and keep his requirements,
his decrees, his laws and his commands always.....
Fix these words of mine in your hearts and minds;
tie them as symbols on your hands
and bind them on your foreheads.

Teach them to your children,
talking about them when you sit at home
and when you walk along the road,
when you lie down and when you get up.
Write them on the doorframes of your houses
and on your gates...

~ Deuteronomy 11:1, 18-20

Painting by Carl Heinrich Bloch (1834–1890)

And he took bread, gave thanks and broke it,
and gave it to them, saying,
*"This is my body given for you;
do this in remembrance of me."*

In the same way, after the supper
he took the cup, saying,
*"This cup is the new covenant in my blood,
which is poured out for you."*

~ Luke 22:19-20

Granddaughter Christine Andersen, Marion, IL

COME TO THE TABLE

During vacation one year, we went as a family to Michigamme Family Camp the second week of August, which is at the peak of the wild blueberry season in the north woods. Several of the campers went out picking blueberries and gave them to our cook. She made wild blueberry muffins which fulfilled two purposes: That evening we ate some with our evening meal. Later that night, we were to have our traditional communion service, but someone forgot to bring the elements. Communion was served using wild blueberry muffins and Orange Crush soda. Our communion that night may not have been typical, but it fit into the geographic area and the time of the year.

> ...The Lord Jesus, on the night he was betrayed, took bread, and when he had given thanks, he broke it and said, *"This is my body, which is for you; do this in remembrance of me."* In the same way, after supper he took the cup, saying, *"This cup is the new covenant in my blood; do this, whenever you drink it, in remembrance of me."* (1 Corinthians 11:23-25)

Jesus is asking us to establish the tradition of taking communion together and, as often as we do it, to remember the sacrifice He made for us. In the previous devotional, one question for discussion was: *"How would you define an empty tradition?"* My witty husband jokingly said, *"The Easter basket on Monday morning."* One of my friends, however, (Rhonda Anderson in Michigan) came up with a good example: *"Christmas without Jesus!"* I believe another empty tradition would be to take communion without remembering Jesus' sacrifice.

According to the Scripture below, the ordinance of the Last Supper is a time to examine ourselves. Although not easy to understand, it brings to light the profound importance of the Eucharist.

> *Whoever, therefore, eats the bread or drinks the cup of the Lord in an unworthy manner will be answerable for the body and blood of the Lord. Examine yourselves, and only then eat of the bread and drink of the cup. For all who eat and drink without discerning the body, eat and drink judgment against themselves.*
> (1 Corinthians 11:27-29 - NRSV)

The Lord's Supper was established by Jesus for our benefit. When we *come to the table,* He meets us there! Yes, it is a time to reflect on our lives, but it is also a time to remember that God loved us so much that He sent His only Son. It is a time of renewal and refreshment as He pours out His love into our hearts.

PONDERINGS

~ Read 1 Corinthians 11:20-22. What was happening in the early church that they were eating and drinking the Lord's supper in an *unworthy* manner? What other actions make us unworthy?

~ Why would it be important to take The Lord's Supper *together*?

~ What is the most meaningful communion experience you have ever had? What made it special?

Lord, let my heart ever hunger after and feed upon You, and may my inmost soul be filled with the sweetness of Your savor; may it ever thirst after You, the fountain of life, the fountain of wisdom and knowledge, the fountain of eternal light, the richness of the house of God. Amen.   ~ Saint Bonaventure (1221-1274)

COME TO THE TABLE

Come to the table, my precious child,
That I have prepared for you;
Here you will find the mercy you need
To experience my love anew.

This is my body, the Bread of Life;
Eat it in remembrance of Me.
For I am the One who gave His life
For you on Calvary's tree.

This is my blood, poured out for you
As a sacrifice for sin;
Take and drink of its soul-cleansing power
And invite my Spirit within.

Come to the table, my precious child;
Leave there the stain of your sin.
Go in peace, refreshed and renewed
And ready to begin again.

~ Idella Pearl Edwards

LET THERE BE LIGHT

Thou, whose almighty word
Chaos and darkness heard,
And took their flight;
Hear us, we humbly pray,
And, where the Gospel day
Sheds not its glorious ray,
Let there be light!

Spirit of truth and love,
Life-giving holy Dove,
Speed forth thy flight!
Move on the waters' face
Bearing the gifts of grace,
And, in earth's darkest place,
Let there be light!

~ *Lyrics by John Marriott (1780-1825)*

Aurora Borealis

LET THERE BE LIGHT!

The Aurora Borealis has always fascinated people. The serene beauty of the Northern Lights is actually produced from millions of explosions of magnetic energy. A multitude of colors are displayed: red, yellow, green, blue and violet, but the most common are pale green and pink. The colors appear to dance with each other, giving the sky an eerie glow.

The Menominee Indians believed the lights were giants who were spirits of great fishermen. The Inuit of Alaska thought they were the spirits of the animals they had killed: deer, whales and seals. Still others thought they were reflections in the clouds from campfires.

The first time I saw the Aurora Borealis was at Michigamme Family Camp in the Upper Peninsula of Michigan. We went outside around midnight to look at the stars when it suddenly caught our attention. It was a jaw-dropping moment.

We had a foreign exchange student from Japan at the camp that year named Toyoko. She had already gone to bed that night, but we did not want her to miss out on this spectacular display.

Someone woke her and led her outside to witness the event. Her reaction was one of fear. She was convinced the world was coming to an end. Her limited English, coupled with her fear, made it difficult to persuade her of the true joy of the event. When she finally understood it to be a natural phenomenon, she was overwhelmed with awe.

There are many things in life that should infuse us with awe, and yet we seem to have lost our sense of wonder. We take everyday miracles for granted. Light is one of them. Light plays an important role in Scripture. On the very first day of creation (Genesis 1:3), God said, *"Let there be light."* In Romans 13:12, the Apostle Paul asks us to *"put aside the deeds of darkness and put on the armor of light."* In John 9:5, Jesus said, *"I am the Light of the World."*

Those thoughts should continue to amaze us, but our sense of wonder has been dulled. Have we lost our amazement that the Light of the whole world lives inside us?

God looks into the darkness of our souls and says, *"Let there be light!"* Perhaps it's time to rekindle our awe for a God who shares with us the dancing lights of His Spirit.

PONDERINGS

~ Have you ever experienced dark times? Who turned on the light?

~ Read Ephesians 5:8-9. How do we live as children of light? What benefits are mentioned?

~ Which areas of your spiritual life need enlightening?

Lord, thou hast given us your Word for a light to shine upon our path; grant us so to meditate on that Word, and to follow its teaching, that we may find in it the light that shines more and more until the perfect day; through Jesus Christ our Lord. Amen.

~ Jerome, (342-420)

Photo by Brian R. Jennings, Pittsburgh, PA

O JESUS, LORD OF LIGHT AND GRACE

O Jesus, Lord of light and grace,
Thou brightness of Thy Father's face,
Thou fountain of eternal light
Whose beams disperse the shades of night;

Come, holy sun of heavenly love,
Send down Thy radiance from above,
And to our inmost hearts convey
Thy Holy Spirit's cloudless ray.

O Christ, with each returning morn
Thine image to our hearts is borne;
O may we ever clearly see
Our Saviour and our God in Thee.

~ St. Ambrose, (340-397)

Photo by Janet Hatfield, Middletown, IN

"Darkness cannot drive out darkness:
only light can do that.
Hate cannot drive out hate:
only love can do that."

~ Martin Luther King, Jr. (1929-1968)

Photo by Tauna Kobler, Marion, IL

For light I go directly to the Source of light,
Not to any of the reflections.

~ *Peace Pilgrim (1908-1981)*

San Domiano, Golconda, IL

Grandson Sam Edwards
Photo by daughter Kerry Jo Montoya, Yukon, OK

THE GIFT OF MUSIC

We have been given the gift of music,
Created before there was time;
Our God placed the rhythm of the universe
In melodies sublime.

Music releases a spirit of hope.
Like an eagle on powerful wings,
It soars to the very presence of God
As all creation sings.

Our voices blend in harmonies sweet
With myriads of angels above;
The saints of the past join in to create
A mighty chorus of love.

Start the drums, the strings and the trumpet;
Let the glorious music begin.
But the very best part comes from the heart,
For the Music Maker lives within.

~ Idella Pearl Edwards

Esther   Harmonica duet with
Great-granddaughter Meghan Malone

GOD GIVES A SONG

I grew up with music.

Until my mother's death in 2009, every family gathering consisted of sing-alongs and concerts. We were always amused that my mother expected the young people to know all the old songs. She would play a song from the 40's and ask the teenagers if they knew the name of it. When they replied "No," she always responded with an incredulous, "You don't???"

Mother was a talented pianist and also played the harmonica, organ, accordion and Hawaiian guitar. On her 100th birthday, she played a concert at church. A portion of the concert can be found on YouTube by searching for "Century Old Esther Edwards."

I grew up hearing music in our home, but it wasn't until I accepted Christ into my heart at the age of 13 that I had a song in my heart. Now, many years later, that song is still making melody deep inside my soul. Aldous Huxley (1894-1963) said: *"Bach gave us God's word, Mozart gave us God's laughter, Beethoven gave us God's fire. God gave us music that we might pray without words."*

Music played a very important role in Bible times. In fact, the longest book in the Bible, the Book of Psalms, is its song book.

The Psalms were the hymnbook of Old Testament Jews. Music was an integral part of worship and festivals and was even used in battle. I love the Scripture in 2 Chronicles 20:21-22:

> ...*Jehoshaphat appointed men to sing to the LORD and to praise him for the splendor of his holiness as they went out at the head of the army...As they began to sing and praise, the LORD set ambushes against the men who were invading Judah, and they were defeated.*

How could music have that kind of impact? Perhaps because it is impossible to sing praises to God in the midst of problems without having faith in His supreme power. Music has power to inspire us, heal us and calm our troubled soul. Martin Luther (1483-1546) said, *"Beautiful music is the art of the prophets that can calm the agitations of the soul; it is one of the most magnificent and delightful presents God has given us."*

If we find our spiritual lives out of tune, it may be from lack of use. I've always heard that a violin that is not used will "go to sleep." The strings on a frequently used violin are more likely to stay in tune. The best way to stay in tune with our Creator and prevent our spiritual life from "going to sleep" is to put His Word into daily practice. When we do, God gives us a song!

PONDERINGS

~ What does music mean to you?

~ Was there a time when you lost your song? What or who helped you get it back?

~ Where do we find our song in the midst of trials?

O God, my heart is steadfast; I will sing and make music. Awake, my soul! Awake, harp and lyre! I will awaken the dawn. I will praise you, O Lord, among the nations; I will sing of you among the peoples. Amen.   (Psalm 57:7-9)

GOD GIVES A SONG

"By the rivers of Babylon, there we sat down and wept, when we remembered Zion.. Upon the willows in the midst of it we hung our harps." Psalms 137:1-2

Words and Music:
Idella Edwards

Arrangement:
Sharon Disney

Though sor-rows try to weigh us down, our con-fi-dence dis-troy, Our
Temp-ta-tion flies from ev-'ry side, En-tic-ing our de-sire, But
Though Sa-tan prowls like a roar-ing lion, And threat-ens to de-vour, Our

God a-bove sends forth His love, And fills our hearts with joy! Don't
God is there with lov-ing care, To shield us from the fire!
God is King o'er ev-'ry thing; He gives us strength and pow'r!

Refrain

hang your harps on the wil-low tree as though all hope is gone, Let the

mel-o-dies roll from the depths of your soul. Our God still gives a song.

Copyright 2003 Idella Pearl Edwards
All rights reserved.

123

THIS DAY

THIS DAY is the first day of the rest of my life;
I will NOT squander it away.
When put to the test, I'll choose God's best
Because I'm thankful for THIS DAY.

THIS DAY is important! It matters what I do!
It could change the rest of my life,
Bringing me peace and love and joy
Or bringing me anger and strife.

THIS DAY is a time to renew my mind
By reading God's Holy Word;
I'll open my heart and let the Spirit reveal
What is pleasing and perfect and good.

THIS DAY I will pray for the hurting and lost,
Taking time to intercede;
I will pray and also put feet to my prayers
To help those who are in need.

THIS DAY I will worship the God of all gods,
Giving praise to His Holy Name;
For He has redeemed me, made me His own.
I'll never be the same.

~ *Idella Pearl Edwards*

"What day is it.?" asked Pooh.
"It's today." squeaked Piglet.
"My favorite day." said Pooh.

TODAY IS THE DAY

Benjamin Franklin once said, *"Don't put off until tomorrow what you can do today."* This is good advice for those of us who tend to procrastinate.

I asked some friends what they procrastinate on most. Here are a few of the results: Rev. Ray Long...household chores; Kim Davis... wrapping gifts, putting away laundry; Brad Edwards... sleep; Donna Cox...starting that diet and exercise program; Rhonda Anderson...projects of any kind, packing for trips; Tara Petrey-Carpenter...phone calls (hate being on hold forever); Jodi Reinhart...pulling weeds; Jo Sanders...raking leaves.

When we procrastinate, we squander that precious asset called time. Procrastination can become a lifestyle. So, why do we procrastinate? Some look for the thrill of the last minute rush. Others avoid a task for fear of failure. Some are lazy. Or perhaps, if they don't make a decision, it absolves them of responsibility for the outcome. Whatever the reason, most procrastinators lie to themselves, saying: *"I'll feel more like doing this later," "I work best under pressure"* or *"It isn't really that important."*

The unfortunate part of foot-dragging is that there are undesirable consequences. These consequences can affect our physical health, our finances and even our relationships. Benjamin Franklin gave some good advice: *"Do you love life? Then do not squander time, for that is the stuff life is made of."* Mother Teresa said, *"Yesterday is gone. Tomorrow has not yet come. We have only today. Let us begin."*

There are some decisions that should never be postponed. If we are not careful, life has a way of passing us by, leaving us with the consequences of our poor choices. Each minute of our time is a gift from God and to be used wisely. Using it wisely, however, does not mean filling every minute with productivity. There are times when the wisest thing to do is rest. If we ask Him, God will lead us in the very best use of our time.

"Look carefully then how you walk, not as unwise but as wise, making the best use of the time, because the days are evil. Therefore do not be foolish, but understand what the will of the Lord is." (Ephesians 5:15-17)

TODAY is the day!

PONDERINGS

~ Is procrastination a learned behavior, or does it come naturally?

~ William A. Ward said, *"God gave you a gift of 86,400 seconds today. Have you used one to say 'thank you?'"* What does this tell us about our use of time?

~ What problems has procrastination caused you in the past? What are you procrastinating about right now?

Lord, may we encourage one another daily, as long as it is called Today, so that none of us may be hardened by sin's deceitfulness. Amen (Based on Hebrews 3:13)

THIS DAY AT THY CREATING WORD

This day at thy creating Word
First o'er the earth the light was poured:
O Lord, this day upon us shine
And fill our souls with light divine.

This day the Lord for sinners slain
In might victorious rose again:
O Jesus, may we raisèd be
From death of sin to life in thee!

This day the Holy Spirit came
With fiery tongues of cloven flame:
O Spirit, fill our hearts this day
With grace to hear and grace to pray.

~ William Walsham How (1823-1897)

WHOLENESS
~ Sarah Martin

(Poem in circle): GAVE my everything to the Great I AM - LAMB of God please come to my SOUL - WHOLE is what I long to BE - SEE the love and joyfully SIGH - I could dance on the crest of an ocean WAVE -

My friend Sarah from Yukon, Oklahoma, wrote this poem as a young teen. Sarah requested that I put the words in a circle because it best represents the completeness of the whole. Sarah's longing to be WHOLE should be ours as well. God doesn't want just a piece of us. He wants us to give our EVERYTHING to The Great I Am.

WHOLE

There are times when a fraction of something is not good enough. No one wants a puzzle with missing pieces. For the gift to be meaningful, they need the *whole* puzzle. We don't want to be 50% healed from cancer, and we would rather not have the termites in our home only 95% controlled. If it rains, and we close all the windows except one, we will still get wet.

Sometimes our lives are that way. We don't feel whole. We feel incomplete. We feel broken. We feel like something is missing. As a child, I always felt broken. I was shy, overweight and poor, which made me feel like an outcast at school.

When I was 13, a friend invited me to Sunday School at her church. I started attending because they had lucky seat numbers and whoever happened to sit on one could win a prize. One Sunday, I noticed a poster advertising a concert by a handsome male quartet from Olivet Nazarene College. I attended the evening service not to hear the message, but to see these handsome young men. God, however, had other plans. The message I heard that evening told me that Jesus could make me whole.

I knelt at the altar in that little storefront church in Aurora, Illinois on September 27, 1953 and gave my heart to Jesus. He filled all the empty places in my life and for the first time, I felt complete. I now belonged to Someone who loved me just the way I was and had a plan for my future. The other church members surrounded me with love and even though our pastor (Rev. Burdetta Lepley) moved to another state the following year, she wrote to me for several years, encouraging me in my newfound faith.

Even in our Christian lives, we sometimes feel incomplete; usually because we have settled for less than God's best. Perhaps we have become lazy in our pursuit of excellence. Some companies dream up slogans to remind their employees of the importance of quality. At Rolls Royce, the slogan was, *"Good enough isn't good enough!"* It reminds us that the race for excellence has no finish line. Perhaps *our* slogan should be Ecclesiastes 9:10, *"Whatever your hand finds to do, do it with all your might..."*

Most importantly, God wants our WHOLE devotion. We will never accomplish His perfect will in our own strength, but God's power can make both our efforts and our spirits WHOLE!

PONDERINGS

~ Have you ever felt incomplete or broken? Why?

~ Read Philippians 3:12-16. Describe your pursuit of spiritual WHOLENESS. Share your successes and failures.

~ John Wesley (1703-1791) said, *"I want the WHOLE Christ for my Savior, the WHOLE Bible for my book, the WHOLE Church for my fellowship, and the WHOLE world for my mission field."* What might change if all Christians adopted this philosophy?

Lord, with my WHOLE heart I have sought You; Oh, let me not wander from Your commandments! Amen.
(Psalm 119:10 NKJV)

All the broken and dislocated pieces
of the universe,
people and things, animals and atoms,
get properly fixed and fit together
in vibrant harmonies,
all because of his death,
his blood that poured down
from the Cross.

~ Colossians 1:20 (MSG)

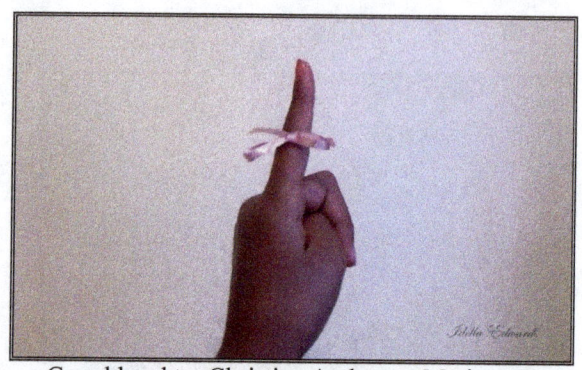

Granddaughter Christine Andersen, Marion, IL

THINGS TO REMEMBER

Does life have a way of getting you down,
Making you angry, making you frown?
Does your strength flee ere the day's half done,
Draining your hope and stealing your song?

Do you find yourself weeping at night on your bed,
Your heart full of sorrow, your soul filled with dread?
It's time to remember that God's in control;
He's your rock, your fortress, the anchor of your soul.

He called you from darkness to His wonderful light;
He has called you to faith in His power and might.
Remember He loves you! Remember He cares!
His strong arms surround you, each burden He bears.

It's time to stand tall; He has made you His own;
You are God's temple and heir to His throne.
So straighten your shoulders and lift up your chin;
You are a royal priesthood for Him.

He who began a good work in you
Will finish the job and see you through.
It's time to remember that God will supply;
For YOU are the apple of His eye.

~ Idella Pearl Edwards

Esther, 1925

I REMEMBER

In 2009, my mother, Esther, died at the age of 100. She had previously made a list of historical events that happened during her lifetime. She entitled it, "Things I Remember."

- 1918 I was 10 years old. World-wide influenza epidemic, infecting 500 million people. Nearly 20 million are dead in U.S. alone.
- 1921 Congress formally ends World War 1.
- 1924 Leopold & Loeb – convicts. Loeb killed by fellow prisoner.
- 1927 Charles Lindberg flies from New York to Paris. First successful solo flight.
- 1929 First phase of depression. We lived in Aurora, Illinois. Herbert Hoover was president.
- 1931 Gangster Al Capone sentenced to 11 years for tax evasion.
- 1933 Chicago Mayor Cermak assassinated.
- 1934 Dionne quintuplets are born in Canada.
- 1937 Amelia Earhart lost somewhere in Pacific on all around the world flight.
- 1941 Japanese surprise attack on Pearl Harbor brings United States into World War Two.
- 1945 Germany surrenders. August 1st - atomic bombs dropped on Hiroshima and Nagasaki – Japan surrenders.

1955 Martin Luther King Jr. leads black boycott of Montgomery, Alabama bus system.

1957 Russians launch Sputnik 1 – first earth orbiting satellite.

1958 United States launches first satellite into orbit - Explorer 1.

1961 First United States spaceman, Alan Shepard, rockets up 116.5 miles. Virgil Grissom, 2nd astronaut, flies 118 miles high.

1962 Lt. John Glenn. First American to orbit earth 3 times.

1963 President Kennedy assassinated in Dallas, Texas. Lee Harvey Oswald accused, then assassinated by Jack Ruby. I saw it happen on TV!

1965 Martin Luther King, Jr. and 2000 blacks arrested in Selma, Alabama about voter registration rules.

1967 Virgil (Gus) Grissom, Edward White and Roger Chaffee killed in spacecraft fire.

1968 Martin Luther King assassinated in Memphis. Senator Robert Kennedy assassinated in Los Angeles.

1969 Neil Armstrong, Edwin "Buzz" Aldrin and Michael Collins – first walk on the moon.

1974 President Nixon resigns after Watergate scandal.

1974 Patricia Hearst kidnapped.

1976 Nation celebrates Bicentennial.

1982 Princess Grace of Monaco, dies after car plunges off mountain road. Her daughter, 7, received serious injuries.

1983 2nd space shuttle, Challenger makes successful maiden voyage. First U.S. space work in 9 years. Sally Ride, 32, first woman astronaut.

1986 Challenger explodes after launch at Cape Canaveral, killing 7.

1991 U.S. forces win Gulf War with Iraq.

1994 Jacqueline Onassis dies – formerly Jackie Kennedy. O.J. Simpson arrested for killing his wife.

1995 Scores killed as car bomb explodes near Oklahoma City's Federal Building, April 19th, Timothy McVeigh, 27, arrested.

1996 Cloning of sheep stirs ethical controversy.

1997 Princess Diana killed in car crash. Mother Teresa dies at 87.

2001 September 11th - terrorists in two airplanes struck the World Trade Towers and they collapsed. Another plane struck the Pentagon and a fourth plane crashed.

2005 Hurricane Katrina killed almost 2000 people on the Gulf Coast.

The list above, of course, is only a tiny fraction of the memories that my mother accumulated over the course of her 100 years. She always had a sharp memory, but she was also fully aware that some things in life are more important to remember than others. The most important thing to remember is God. Throughout the Bible, it always pleased the Lord for people to remember Him, and it made Him sad when they forgot Him. In Jeremiah 2:32 (NLT), God said, *"Does a young woman forget her jewelry? Does a bride hide her wedding dress? No! Yet for years on end my people have forgotten me."*

We are to remember God. The Bible tells us it is the most difficult to remember God when things are going well. *"When you eat and are satisfied, when you build fine houses and settle down, and when your herds and flocks grow large and your silver and gold increase and all you have is multiplied, then your heart will become proud and you will forget the LORD your God..."* (Deuteronomy 8:12-14) God yearns to hear you say, "I REMEMBER!"

PONDERINGS

~ Do you tend to remember the good memories or the bad ones? Share one of your favorite good memories with the group.

~ Read Psalm 103:12 and Malachi 3:16. What does this tell you about what God remembers?

~ What are the disadvantages of being forgetful? What are some good ways to refresh your memory?

I confess, Lord, with thanksgiving that you have made me in your image, so that I can remember you, think of you, and love you. Amen.   ~ St. Anselm (1033-1109)

Do you remember the things you were worrying about a year ago? How did they work out? Didn't you waste a ton of fruitless energy on account of most of them? Didn't most of them turn out all right after all?
~ Dale Carnegie (1888-1955)

ESTHER

Only be careful, and watch yourselves closely so that you do not forget the things your eyes have seen or let them slip from your heart as long as you live…
~ Deuteronomy 4:9

ROSES ARE RED

Several years ago, since I am a poet, I encouraged my family (5 kids and 12 grandkids) to write a poem for me. It seems that anytime poetry is mentioned, the poem "Roses Are Red" always comes to mind. *"Roses are red, violets are blue, sugar is sweet, and so are you."* The origin of this poem dates back as far as 1590 to a similar poem written by Sir Edmund Spenser.

It was inevitable that, in addition to some really great poems, several family members decided to create their own rendition of the "Roses Are Red" poem. Our grandson Joe and my husband Jack both went in that direction.

MY POEM

Violets are blue
Kool-Aid is red
I like fried chicken
And corn bread

~ Joseph Montoya

FOOD FOR THOUGHT

Pumpkins are orange.
Radishes are red.
Peas are green.
Having a rough time.
This doesn't rhyme!

Bananas are yellow.
Plums are purple.
Blueberries are blue.
Wife could do better.
Guess I'll let her!

~ Jack Griffis Edwards

Roses, of course, come in a multitude of colors, but the red rose is rich in history, representing love and romance. Robert Burns wrote a song in 1794 that proclaims *"My love is like a red, red rose."* The red rose also stands for respect and courage, and was adopted as a symbol of the blood of the Christian martyrs.

God's love is like a red, red rose! God sent the Red Rose of His great love in the form of His only Son. Yes, *"Roses are red, violets are blue, sugar is sweet, and GOD LOVES YOU!"*

PONDERINGS

~ What's your favorite color? It has been said that the color "red" motivates us to take action. Do you agree?

~ Do you feel more loved when someone gives you a gift? How can we help people appreciate God's gift of His Son?

~ Read 2 Corinthians 2:15. How are we like a rose?

Lord, we thank you for our senses by which we hear the songs of birds, and see the splendor of fields of golden wheat, and taste autumn's fruit, rejoice in the feel of snow, and smell the breath of spring flowers. Amen.   ~ Walter Rauschenbusch (1861–1918)

Grandson Zac Benson, Sandusky, OH

I FOUND A TREASURE

Our grandson, Zac, was very pleased to find a colorful stone on the lakeshore. He was very proud of his "treasure." We all like treasures. Our evaluation of what constitutes a real treasure may change over the course of our lifetime, but we still enjoy the fantasy of finding and owning something valuable.

When I was a child, I had a recurring dream about finding a treasure. In my dream, I would climb over a high fence and on the other side I would start digging with my little shovel. I would dig a deep hole, discovering a large pile of coins – quarters, dimes, nickels and pennies. Then I would sit beside the hole, scoop up the coins in my hands, lift them high over my head and allow them to cascade down on top of me. I never spent any of the money or took it home. In my dream, I just enjoyed the pleasure of finding the treasure.

Everyone seems to have a different idea as to what constitutes a treasure. When our son, Bruce, moved to Indiana, one of his new friends gave him free reign to salvage anything he wanted in an old house before it was to be destroyed. Here is Bruce's response:

What a treasure!!! A good friend here in our new town manages a trucking terminal on whose property exists an old house. They were just going to burn it down, but since I have a workshop they decided to give me a crack at salvaging some building materials. The house has a slew of old oak plank trim, cabinets for my workshop, light fixtures, window air conditioners, etc, etc, etc.

A friend of Bruce's responded to his announcement: *"What a great project for someone like you who has the knowledge, the industriousness and the ability to see future usefulness and beauty in what most folks would think was just old wood."*

Bruce's heart and passion was in this project. The Bible tells us that "...*w*here your treasure is, there your heart will be also." (Matthew 6:21) God wants us to be passionate about our life here on earth, but even more so, He desires that we be passionate about HIS treasure. God's treasure is Jesus.

What is truly a treasure? Are God's treasures OUR treasures? All the treasures of this world are worth nothing without Jesus. God also sees US as His treasure. He has the ability to see the future usefulness and beauty in each one of us.

PONDERINGS

~ If earthly treasurers are inferior to heavenly ones, why are they so tempting?

~ If someone observed your life, what would they name as your ultimate treasure? How could they tell?

~ What might be some warning signs that we are building up earthly treasures?

Lord, while we gratefully receive the gifts of your bounty, let us not incur the guilt of loving the creature more than the Creator, or of laying up treasure on earth to the neglect of our treasure in heaven. Amen.   ~ Morning and Evening prayers (1574)

The kingdom of heaven
is like treasure hidden in a field.
When a man found it,
he hid it again, and then in his joy
went and sold all he had
and bought that field.

(Matthew 13:44)

THE BUMBLEBEE
~ Written in honor of Thelma Wells,
Speaker for Women of Faith

The bumblebee does not have a clue
That he shouldn't be able to fly
His robust body, borne by tiny wings
Easily soars to the sky.

My faith has sprouted tiny wings
But unlike the bumblebee,
I tend to focus on their size
And ignore God's power in me.

Lord, teach me to fly on wings of faith
And know that I am free
To rise above my doubt and fear
And be all I can be.

Yes, my wings are very small,
Just like the bumblebee's,
But God fills each wing with holy power
When I linger on my knees.

~ *Idella Pearl Edwards*

Photo by son Bruce Edwards, Bloomfield, IN

BEE YOUR BEST

I have attended the Women of Faith Conferences several times. There are many great speakers but I have always been impressed with Thelma Wells, who is also known as "Mama T" or "The Bumblebee Lady". (She has a whole line of bumblebee jewelry.) In her presentation, she told us, *"The bumblebee's wings are too small to support its robust body, so technically it cannot fly. But the bumblebee doesn't know that, so it flies anyway."*

Thelma uses the bumblebee to represent overcoming life's obstacles. Her motto is, *"In Christ, you can BEE your best!"* As a child, she overcame many obstacles. Born to a crippled, unwed teenager, she was raised by her great-grandparents. They took her to church where she learned to love the hymns and praise songs.

Occasionally, she spent time with her grandmother who abused her by locking her in a dark, insect-infested closet for hours at a time. Thelma spent her time in the closet singing all the songs she had learned in church. In her 70's, she was still conducting women's conferences and retreats and writing books. She has been married to her best friend, George Wells, for over 50 years and resides in Dallas, Texas.

When we are not at our best, we are very adept at blaming our circumstances. We use every excuse we can find for failing to reach our goals. We feel our financial or health or relationship problems give us valid reasons for not BEE-ing our best, so we bemoan the fact that we cannot reach our goals, and we settle in for one big pity party.

2 Timothy 2:15 encourages us to be our best: *"Do your best to present yourself to God as one approved, a workman who does not need to be ashamed and who correctly handles the word of truth."*

The bumblebee does not sit around and complain about the size of its wings. It has a job to do, and God gave it everything it needs to do that job. He gave each of us a job to do as well and, *"His divine power has given us everything we need for life and godliness through our knowledge of him who called us by his own glory and goodness."* (2 Peter 1:3) That's the only way we can BEE our best!

PONDERINGS

~ Ralph Waldo Emerson (1803-1882) said, *"Make the most of yourself, for that is all there is of you."* How do we motivate ourselves to go above and beyond our mediocre expectations?

~ Harriet Beecher Stowe (1811-1896) said, *"When you get into a tight place and everything goes against you, till it seems as though you could not hang on a minute longer, never give up then, for that is just the place and time that the tide will turn."* Have you ever experienced this? When?

~ Are there any areas or tasks that you have not really taken seriously and need to work on?

O Lord, help us to discern what is best that we might be pure and blameless and filled with the fruit of righteousness. Amen.
(Based on Philippians 1:10-11)

"THE BUMBLEBEE LADY"

Thelma Wells (photo used by permission)

www.thelmawells.com

"Jesus Wept" statue, erected a few hundred feet from the Oklahoma City bomb site.

Alfred P. Murrah Federal Building, Oklahoma City, OK

DISASTER

My husband, Jack, worked for the Department of Transportation in Oklahoma City during the time of the bombing disaster. He shares the following:

April 19, 1995 is a date that is permanently etched into my mind. That morning I was in my pickup with the radio playing on my way to the airport terminal to pick up a package. A news bulletin came over the radio that at 9:02 AM, a bomb had detonated in front of the Alfred P. Murrah Federal Building in downtown Oklahoma City. The early report stated that the entire front half of the building collapsed.

I made a U-turn in the middle of the street and headed back to my office located on the western airport property. A very short time after returning to my office, I received a call from our Washington D.C. office asking me to serve as the informational go-between for the Federal agencies in Washington D.C. and those in Oklahoma City. I served in this temporary assignment for about a week.

The final count of casualties included 168 deaths (19 of which were children) and over 800 injured. I lost one co-worker.

This was an experience neither my husband nor I will ever forget. The blast damaged 324 buildings, 86 cars and shattered glass in over 250 nearby buildings. Walking downtown afterwards gave us the eerie feeling of being in a war zone in a foreign country. Visiting the Oklahoma City National Memorial (built a few years later) is a very emotional experience.

Why did this happen? Where was security? The problem was that a harmless-looking Ryder rental van sat outside the building. No one suspected what was inside!

It is the same with our lives. Perhaps Ralph Waldo Emerson's statement can apply both to the positive and the negative aspects of our lives: *"What lies behind you and what lies in front of you, pales in comparison to what lies inside of you."* We sometimes carry around explosive cargo as well. The Bible explicitly tells us to get rid of it! *"Get rid of all bitterness, rage and anger, brawling and slander, along with every form of malice."* (Colossians 3:8) If we let God work on us from the inside out, our lives will not become a disaster.

PONDERINGS

~ What is the danger of allowing anger, bitterness, fear or envy to fester inside of us? How do we overcome evil with good?

~ Read Galatians 5:22-23. Look at each attribute. Which one do we need to cultivate the most?

~ We sometimes feel powerless to change the inside of ourselves. Read Matthew 19:26. How do we increase our faith in God's power to change us from the inside out?

O Almighty God, help us to put away all bitterness and wrath and evil-speaking, with all malice. May we possess our souls in patience, however we are tempted and provoked, and not be overcome with evil, but overcome evil with good. Amen.

~ Benjamin Jenks (1646-1724)

God is our refuge and strength, an ever-present help in trouble.

~ Psalm 46:1

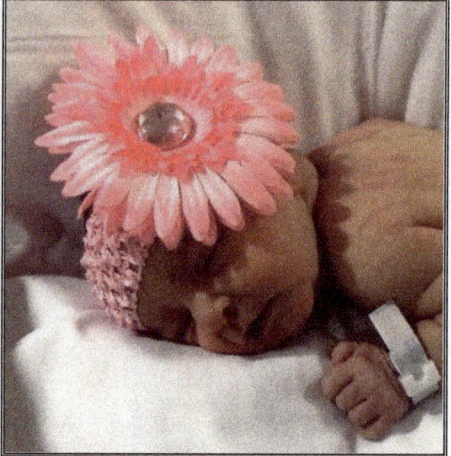

Teagan Bell Cosby
Granddaughter of Rev. and Mrs. Stan Cosby, Amarillo, TX

WHAT A BABY COSTS

For babies people have to pay
A heavy price from day to day -
There is no way to get one cheap
Why, sometimes when they're fast asleep
You have to get up in the night
And go and see that they're alright.
But what they cost in constant care
And worry, does not half compare
With what they bring of joy and bliss -
You'd pay much more for just a kiss.

~ Edgar Guest (1881-1959)

Eli, Grace and Sophia Hope Carpenter
Photo by Sylvia Petrey, Norman, OK

BEHOLD, I MAKE ALL THINGS NEW

We all like new things. New cars, new clothes and even a brand new day. But is there anything sweeter than a newborn baby? Joy and pride can be seen on the faces of both big brother and big sister above. God said, "...*Behold, I make all things new.*" (Revelation 21:5)

I remember well the thrill of having a brand new baby. Each time I gave birth, it was the same….a feeling of awe as I marveled at God's miraculous creation and a feeling of endless gratitude for the gift of life placed in my arms.

When I think back to those days, the memories that stand out are not the ones of lost sleep or dirty diapers. The treasured memories are the ones of counting each tiny, miraculous finger or toe of the cuddly warm body snuggled next to mine, and I vividly remember melting in the presence of that very first smile.

God specializes in the new. *"Any one who is in Christ is a new creation, the old has gone and the new has come."* (2 Corinthians 5:17) Ephesians 4:22-24 tells us, *"You were taught, with regard to your former way of life, to put off your old self, which is being corrupted by its deceitful desires; to be made new in the attitude of your minds; and to put on the new self, created to be like God in true righteousness and holiness."*

God is able to radically transform us from the inside out. It doesn't matter what we have done in the past or how many times we have failed. He wants us to let go of old hurts and bad experiences. He even encourages us to put aside the old, limited expectations of our talents and abilities.

God longs to do something new in our lives. He desires to use His power to develop the potential for which He created us. Can you hear him? He is saying, *"Behold I make ALL things new, and that includes you!"*

PONDERINGS

~ Are you stuck in the past? What past mistakes or experiences seem to drag you down? What do you see when you view your life? Do you see problems or possibilities?

~ What did Mark Twain mean by this statement? *"You will be more disappointed by the things that you didn't do than by the ones you did do. Sail away from the safe harbor. Catch the trade winds in your sails. Explore. Dream. Discover."*

~ What "new" thing might God want to do in your life? How can you prepare for it?

Lord, we call this to mind and therefore we have hope. Because of Your great love, we are not consumed for Your compassions never fail. They are NEW every morning. Great is Your faithfulness. Amen. (Based on Lamentations 3:21-24)

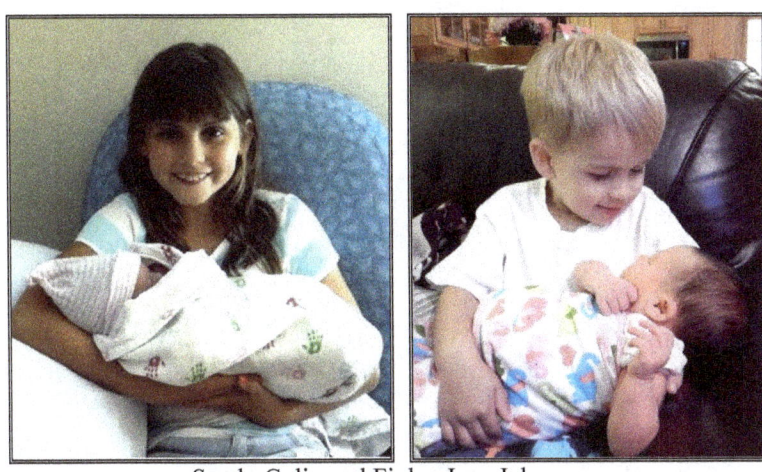

Sarah, Colin and Finley Jean Johnson
Photos by Ken Johnson, Sugar Grove, IL

A baby is God's opinion that life should go on.
~ *Carl Sandburg (1878-1967)*

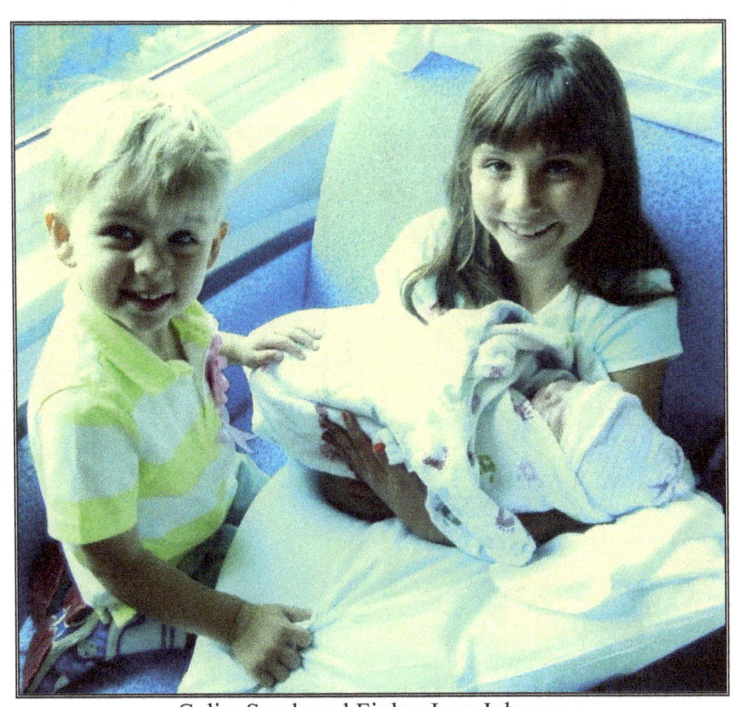

Colin, Sarah and Finley Jean Johnson

Brad Ben Ben

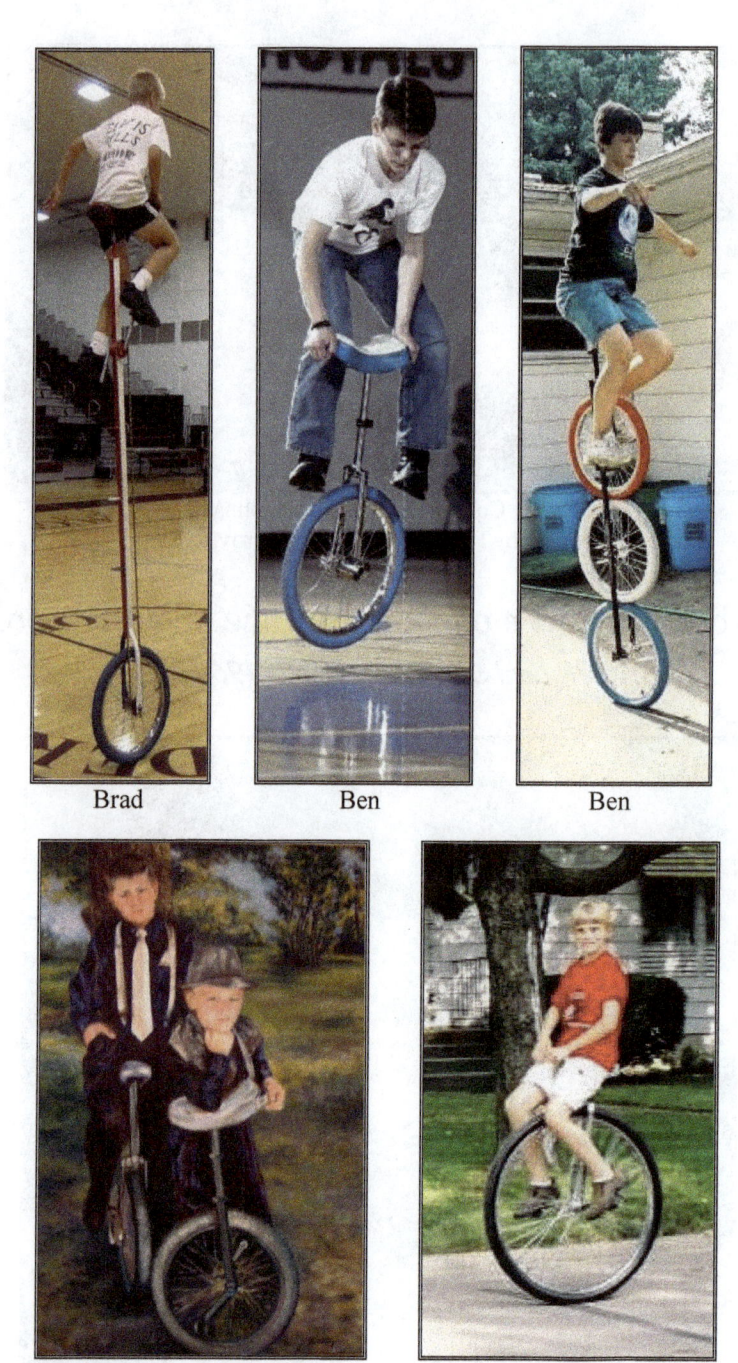

Grandsons Ben & Brad Edwards
Painting by daughter Kerry Jo Montoya

Brad on a Coker Unicycle

"Clyde" and grandson Ben Edwards

ONE IS ENOUGH

There are many times in life when ONE is *not* enough. ONE cookie never seems to be enough. ONE tooth has its disadvantages. ONE bedroom may not be enough if you have six children. In fact, quite often, ONE paycheck does not seem to be enough.

Other times, however, ONE is more than enough. Our grandsons, Ben and Brad, learned very early in life that they did not need a bicycle to get around. After they each learned how to ride a unicycle, they discovered that ONE wheel was more than enough. Since that time, they have competed and won several awards in unicycling competitions and have also enjoyed riding in many parades. Their father also competed on a unicycle. Our son, Bruce, shares the following:

> In a midlife crisis event, I bought a unicycle for my 40th birthday and learned to ride it. I have since competed at the national level in the sport of unicycling, riding in the one-mile off-road race at the National Championships in Minneapolis in

2003. Results? I did not get last place because I beat two six-year-old girls who got lost in the woods.

Regardless of the results, the ONE wheel of the unicycle was more than enough to bring Bruce great satisfaction and enjoyment. He says that when he rides a unicycle, he has "one wheely" good time. Yes, for some things, ONE is enough.

The Bible has a great deal to say about the number ONE. Ephesians 4:4-6 tells us, *"There is ONE body and ONE Spirit - just as you were called to ONE hope when you were called - ONE Lord, ONE faith, ONE baptism; ONE God and Father of all, who is over all and through all and in all."* 1 Timothy 2:5 is very clear that there is only ONE way to God and that is through His Son, Jesus: *"For there is ONE God and ONE mediator between God and men, the man Christ Jesus."*

When it comes to Jesus, ONE is enough! He is all we need to find forgiveness and eternal life!

PONDERINGS

~ Do you have any desire to ride a unicycle? Are there other things in life that you would like to do but are afraid to try?

~ What are some of the little "gods" that rob us of our intention to worship the ONE true God?

~ Read John 14:6. Do you agree with this scripture? Why is it often rejected today? Why is it important to insist that Jesus is the only way to heaven?

God, out of Thy Goodness, give me Thyself: for Thou art enough for me. If I desire anything less, I find myself in want. In Thee alone I have all. To Thee be glory and honor, dominion and power, now and ever more. Amen.   ~ Julian of Norwich (1342-1416)

Son Bruce Edwards, Bloomfield, IN

Grandson Ben Edwards 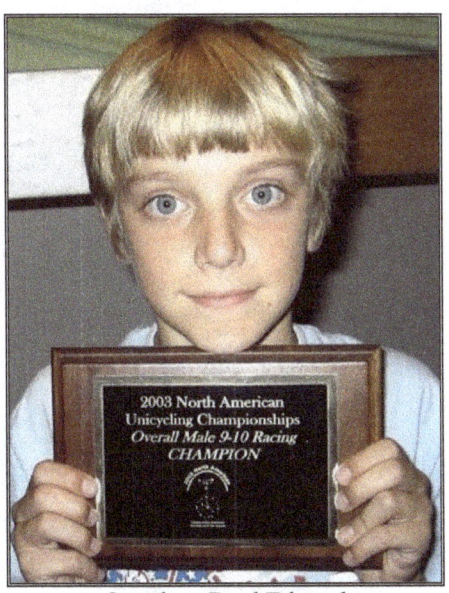   Grandson Brad Edwards

Idella Edwards

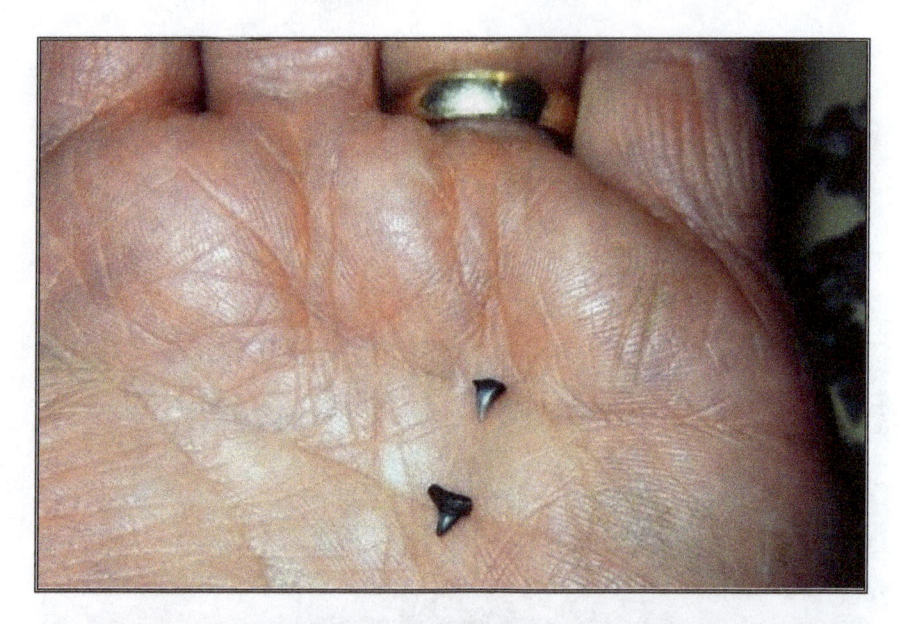

Photo by son Bruce Edwards, Bloomfield, IN

PUT SOME TEETH INTO IT

The expression, "*put some teeth into it*", means to increase the power of something. To see the real power of the teeth in the photo above, they would somehow have to be put back into the shark's mouth. Sharks may have up to 3000 teeth at one time. They are arranged in rows and most sharks have about five rows of teeth. A shark attack on a human can do great damage. The initial bite can sever a limb completely. They really "*put their teeth into it.*" Although there are only about 75 attacks each year, great fear was introduced by the famous horror movie, "Jaws."

When my family lived near the Chesapeake Bay, one of our favorite activities was hunting for shark's teeth along the beach. We usually went at low tide after a storm because that increased the possibilities of more teeth washing up on shore. They came in all sizes, so it was always a contest between family members to see who could find the most and who could find the largest.

The kids also found some very tiny ones and always bragged at what sharp eyes they had to be able to spot them among the rocks. We also enjoyed identifying each tooth as to what kind of shark it came from and also the location in the shark's mouth. The sharks' teeth in the Chesapeake Bay are fossilized teeth from long ago.

There are many times in life when we need to put teeth into something. Some of our laws, for example, could definitely use more teeth. One area, for the Christian, that could use more teeth is our prayer life. How do we make our prayer life more effective? Here is the profound answer...PRAY WITH FAITH! This will put teeth into our prayers! Smith Wigglesworth (1859-1947) said: *"There is something about believing God that will cause Him to pass over a million people to get to you because of your faith."*

How do we increase our faith and the power of our prayers? The best way is to sink our teeth into God's Word. *"God's Word vaults across the skies from sunrise to sunset, melting ice, scorching deserts, warming hearts to faith."* Psalm 19:6 (MSG)

PONDERINGS

~ Read Hebrews 4:16. How is it possible to come "boldly" before God?

~ Read John 10:27. Is your prayer time a two-way conversation? How much time do you spend listening for God's voice?

~ Andrew Murray (1828-1917) said, *"Each time, before you intercede, be quiet first, and worship God in His glory. Think of what He can do, and how He delights to hear the prayers of His redeemed people. Think of your place and privilege in Christ, and expect great things!"* Is this good advice? Why or why not?

Our Father in heaven, Hallowed be Your name. Your kingdom come. Your will be done on earth as it is in heaven. Give us this day our daily bread. And forgive us our debts, as we forgive our debtors. And do not lead us into temptation, but deliver us from the evil one. For Yours is the kingdom and the power and the glory forever. Amen.   (Matthew 6:9-13 NKJV)

Photo by Missionaries John and Colleen Eisenberg, Asunción, Paraguay

PRAYER

Breathing in the Breath of Life
That saturates my soul;
Breathing out the fear and doubt
That block His Kingdom's goal.

Breathing in God's sacred love
That holds me in His care;
Breathing out my loneliness
That leaves me in despair.

Breathing in God's mercy, bowing
'Neath the cleansing flood;
Breathing out the guilt and sin
Now covered by His blood.

Breathing in a bright, clear vision
To help a world in need;
Breathing out my tendencies
Of selfishness and greed.

Breathing in a firm desire
To be all I can be;
Breathing out the status quo
Of mediocrity.

~ *Idella Pearl Edwards*

Granddaughter Colleen Malone and friend Sara Battelle
Photo by daughter Karen Malone, Fenton, MO

CELEBRATE

God spoke the Word and it was done,
Creating land and sea;
And wonder of wonders, in His own image,
He created you and me.

God shouts His love to all the world
From a cross on Calvary.
He writes His word upon our hearts
And sets our spirits free;

God bids us come as a little child
Who delights that the father is near;
He bids us leap with sweet abandon,
Into his loving care.

O celebrate the goodness of God!
What more could He have done?
He demonstrated His great love
Through the gift of His only Son!

~ Idella Pearl Edwards

Grandson Zac Benson, Sandusky, OH

A LEAP OF FAITH

What is faith? The Bible tells us, *"...faith is being sure of what we hope for and certain of what we do not see."* (Hebrews 11:1) Have you ever taken a leap of faith? Sometimes it is difficult to take even baby steps of faith. Although it is not easy, God wants us to, *"...live by faith, not by sight."* (2 Corinthians 5:7)

Many times, God orchestrates events in our lives that shout to us from heaven, saying, *"I am here! I care! I love you! I will take care of you!"* I well remember the anxiety I experienced one time with an upcoming thyroid surgery. Because of two previous throat surgeries, one of which resulted in a serious complication, I began to fantasize about all the negative possibilities. I knew all the right Bible passages such as Psalm 56:3-4, *"When I am afraid, I will trust in you. In God, whose word I praise, in God I trust; I will not be afraid. What can mortal man do to me?"* Even so, I could not calm my anxiety.

I was at the church that week and walked into the sanctuary. The pastor was there, and the youth group was meeting over in one corner. I shared my fears with our pastor. He immediately called the youth group over to lay hands on me and pray. Several young people led out in prayer, and I began to experience a sensation of warmth that spread from my toes to the top of my head. Needless to say, every fear dissipated. When I entered the hospital the next day, my heart was filled with peace as I took a leap of faith and put all my trust in God.

We have a choice: to walk by sight or to walk by faith. Walking by sight is easy and safe, but it doesn't always take us where God wants us to go. Walking by faith can be scary, but also exciting and can take us to places we never dreamed possible. Henry Ward Beecher (1813-1887) said, *"Every tomorrow has two handles. We can take hold of it with the handle of anxiety or the handle of faith."* Only when we are willing to take a leap of faith will we experience God's greatest blessings.

PONDERINGS

~ Louis E. Boon (1941-2005) said: *"Don't fear failure so much that you refuse to try new things. The saddest summary of a life contains three descriptions: could have, might have, and should have."* Do any of those descriptions fit your life?

~ George Mueller also said, *"The beginning of anxiety is the end of faith, and the beginning of true faith is the end of anxiety."* Is this true? Why or why not?

~ Can you remember a time in your life when you took a leap of faith? Share with the group.

O God of grace, increase my faith! Help me to daily trust Thy Word; give me the strength that always comes from leaning on my blessèd Lord. O God of grace, in Jesus' name, increase my faith, upbuild my hope, my heart with zeal inflame. Send down Thy Spirit from above, till faith and hope are lost in love. Amen.
~ Lyrics by Neal A. McAnlay (1897)

Jennifer Andersson, Detroit, MI
Lake Michigan

Sometimes your only
available transportation
is a leap of faith.

~ *Margaret Shepard (1843-1924)*

Granddaughter Christine Andersen, Marion, IL

Photo by Tauna Kobler, Marion, IL

THE ROAD NOT TAKEN

Two roads diverged in a yellow wood,
And sorry I could not travel both
And be one traveler, long I stood
And looked down one as far as I could
To where it bent in the undergrowth;
Then took the other, as just as fair,
And having perhaps the better claim,
Because it was grassy and wanted wear;
Though as for that the passing there
Had worn them really about the same,
And both that morning equally lay
In leaves no step had trodden black.
Oh, I kept the first for another day!
Yet knowing how way leads on to way,
I doubted if I should ever come back.
I shall be telling this with a sigh
Somewhere ages and ages hence:
Two roads diverged in a wood, and I-
I took the one less traveled by,
And that has made all the difference.

~ Robert Frost (1874 - 1963)

> IGLESIA METODISTA DE MÉXICO, A.R.
> MANOS JUNTAS MÉXICO, A.C.
>
> DEDICAN ESTE EDIFICIO EN HONOR A
>
> *Bill & Edra Edwards*
>
> *Por su infatigable labor de amor a la comunidad de Río Bravo.*
>
> Cd. Río Bravo, Tamaulipas., 27 de Febrero de 2014

THE ROAD LESS TRAVELED

My husband's brother and his wife, Bill and Edra Edwards, have been on mission trips all over the world. Even before retirement from their successful professional careers, they put top priority on mission work. In February of 2014, Rio Bravo Hands Together Mission in Mexico dedicated their new Community Center and Clinic to them for 15 years of devoted service. Bill and Edra had many choices in life, but they chose to do what many people would never dream of doing. God called them to take the road less traveled.

God blessed them with several miracles during their years of service. Bill and Edra recently shared the following incident:

> One day after lunch, the van driver took an alternate route back to the work site. He assured the work team he was not lost, but he certainly took a different route than ever before. Suddenly they came to a place in a road where a crowd had gathered. They noticed three women sobbing and saw the blood-covered girl sitting at the curb.
>
> Our team stopped to help. By the grace of God, this construction team had an interpreter, an EMT and a nurse. They noticed an odd shaped lump in the young woman's

trouser leg and through the interpreter asked if she might have given birth. YES! She had begun having contractions and walked a mile and a half to try to get to her mother-in-law, who called emergency. The crowd, however, seemed to have no idea what to do. Our team took charge, sent the hysterical relatives for blankets, started crowd control moving the stunned onlookers back, slit the girl's trousers, removed the baby, untangled the cord and started resuscitation. The mother was in good condition but the bluish baby was a concern.

When the ambulance arrived, the crew turned its full attention on the mother, ignoring the baby. Fortunately our nurse with neonatal experience was tenacious about the care the baby needed and forced the emergency crew to attend to it. Since this was a poor colonia, they were not going to take the patients to the hospital unless they were paid first. So our team took care of that. The mother was released, and the baby girl, after a rough start was also released. Praise God!

Mother and baby were saved because the mission team chose to follow God and take the road less traveled!

PONDERINGS

~ Read Matthew 7:14. Is it possible the narrow road represents our service as well as our salvation? Why or why not?

~ Is missionary work always done in a foreign country? What type of mission work should we be doing here at home?

~ Read Matthew 28:19-20. How are you fulfilling the great commission? In the world? In your community? In your church? In your family?

God, only wise, almighty, good. Send forth thy truth and light,
To point us out the narrow road, and guide our steps aright. Amen.

~ A Collection of Hymns for the Methodist Episcopal Church (1847)

Bill and Edra Edwards, Horseshoe Bay, TX

"If anyone gives even a cup of cold water
to one of these little ones
because he is my disciple,
I tell you the truth,
he will certainly not lose his reward."

~ Matthew 10:42

Goddard Chapel, Marion, IL

I AM THE DOOR

Many are the choices along life's way,
Each with a promise to fulfill;
But only one will satisfy,
Others leave us wanting still.

Each choice is a doorway that bids us enter,
Some promise glitter and gold,
But one Door and only one,
Each promise will uphold.

Don't look left! Don't look right!
Keep your eyes straight ahead.
Only one Door offers life,
Just as Jesus said.

"I am the Way, the Truth, the Life,
Come to the Father through Me;
I am the one and only Door,
Who is able to set you free!"

O Sinner, stand at the Door and knock;
Do not delay your choice!
Jesus will welcome you into His arms
As all heaven's angels rejoice!

~ Idella Pearl Edwards

Dave and Peggy Maragni, Marion, IL

THE OPEN DOOR

Dave and Peggy Maragni are co-owners of The Promise, a ministry in Marion, Illinois that offers hope and love to the homeless and needy. When I first met Dave and Peggy, I was very impressed with their "open door" policy. They welcome anyone and everyone with the love of Jesus regardless of their walk in life.

Peggy shared this on facebook... *"One day a man came in and said, 'I was sent by a men's prayer group and told that you guys would help me to find the Lord.' It's amazing watching God bring people to us. We don't even have to look for them. I pray I never get in Gods way!"*

Dave and Peggy have dedicated their lives to serving others. She said:

> I woke up this morning with a heavy heart, thinking, *"I'm not doing enough at The Promise."* Our goal there is to love on God's children, no matter what their sin is. We never planned to have a food pantry...we wanted a people pantry, but God chose for us to have both. Everything that comes through the front door is ALL God. Dave and I are just servants. Mark 10:45 says, *"The Son of Man did not come to be served, but to*

serve, and to give his life as a ransom for many." I pray Dave and I can reach this goal in our walk at The Promise. Please pray for us every day. God Bless!

God has blessed The Promise through their ministry - sometimes through big miracles - sometimes through small ones. One time, after all our family members returned home after a holiday, my husband Jack decided to take all the leftover sodas to The Promise. Peggy posted this message on Facebook the next day:

> Yesterday was an awesome day. James, who is here every day, brought his girlfriend with him for lunch. During that time someone was dropping off cans of soda, including some Pepsi. Not knowing this, the girlfriend asked James for a Pepsi just as it came through the door. I heard James tell her, *"Anything you ask for always comes through that door!"* LOL. Thank you, Jack, for making this couple happy and helping them to see God in action. Every day at The Promise is a MIRACLE!

Yes, The Promise has an "open door". God loves open doors! Revelation 3:8 tells us, *"...I have placed before you an open door that no one can shut..."*

PONDERINGS

~ A song in the movie, "Frozen," proclaims, "Love Is An Open Door." Is it? What doors do we tend to close on others?

~ Does your church have an open door policy? Which doors should be opened wider?

~ Read Luke 14:12-14. Is Jesus telling us not to have family gatherings? What is the point of this story?

O God, make the door of this house wide enough to receive all who need human love and fellowship, and a heavenly Father's care; and narrow enough to shut out all envy, pride and hate. Make it a gateway to your eternal kingdom. Amen.

~ Thomas Ken (1637-1711)

Granddaughter Jackie Edwards, Everson, WA

"Pray for us, too,
that God may open a door
for our message, so that
we may proclaim
the mystery of Christ..."

~ Colossians 4:3

Clouds come floating into my life,
no longer to carry rain
or usher storm,
but to add color
to my sunset sky.

~ Rabindranath Tagore (1861-1941)

Photo by Tauna Kobler, Marion, IL

THE STORMS OF LIFE

On May 8, 2009, an inland hurricane swept through our town of Marion, Illinois, causing millions of dollars in damage. Fierce winds, reaching 106 miles per hour, snapped trees like matchsticks, peeled siding off homes, blew out car windows and overturned a semi-trailer. Thirty-nine tornadoes were reported in Southern Kansas, Missouri and Illinois. Over 70,000 homes were without power, some for more than a week.

To our advantage, the winds were fickle, and we were blessed to have no damage, but as we watched, our neighbor's roof tiles peeled off and sailed through the air.

Our daughter and family live ½ mile from us, but cell phones were also down, and we could not contact them to see if they were ok. We tried to drive to their home, but could not get through because of large trees across the road. Later, our son-in-law walked over to our house to check on us. My daughter told us that strangers with a baby and a cat had suddenly run into her house and headed straight for the basement.

This side of heaven, we will all experience a few storms. Life can be pleasant and enjoyable but suddenly, when we least expect it, the bottom drops out. For the Christian, there is hope in knowing that God is with us in the midst of our troubles. William Cowper (1731-1800) said, *"God moves in a mysterious way, His wonders to perform. He plants His footsteps in the sea, and rides upon the storm."*

It is through the storms of life that God teaches us how to walk by faith. He wants each of us to become like a little child again, putting our hand in His and knowing that, as long as we are with Him, everything will be all right.

We need not fear the storms of life because... *"God is our refuge and strength, an ever-present help in trouble. Therefore we will not fear, though the earth give way and the mountains fall into the heart of the sea, though its waters roar and foam and the mountains quake with their surging."* (Psalm 46:1-3)

PONDERINGS

~ Read Mark 4:35-41. What is your most frightening "storm" experience? Why were the disciples upset when they found Jesus sleeping?

~ Jesus asked the disciples, *"Why are you so afraid? Do you still have no faith?"* What does faith have to do with fear? Is Psalm 56:3-4 really possible?

~ What current storm are you in right now that you would like the group to pray about?

Our God, our help in ages past, our hope for years to come, our shelter from the stormy blast, and our eternal home. Beneath the shadow of thy throne, thy saints have dwelt secure; sufficient is thine arm alone, and our defense is sure. Amen
~ Isaac Watts (1674-1748)

Inland Hurricane, Marion, IL

Be still, sad heart! And cease repining;
Behind the clouds is the sun still shining;
Thy fate is the common fate of all,
Into each life some rain must fall.

~ Henry Wadsworth Longfellow (1807-1882)

Photo by Janet Hatfield, Middletown, IN

GOD STILLS THE STORM

I cried to the Lord in my troubles;
My courage melting away.
He put His loving arms 'round me,
Giving me strength for the day.

He brought me out of the darkness;
Out of my gloom and despair.
He shared the light of His presence,
In response to my needy prayer.

God stilled the storm to a whisper;
All fear and doubt are gone.
He warms my soul with His sunshine;
He fills my heart with His song.

~ *Idella Pearl Edwards*

*"Then they cried out to the Lord in their trouble,
and he brought them out of their distress.
He stilled the storm to a whisper;
the waves of the sea were hushed."*

Psalm 107:28-29

Waldorf, MD
Photo by son Bruce Edwards, Bloomfield, IN

STOPPING BY WOODS ON A SNOWY EVENING

Whose woods these are I think I know.
His house is in the village, though;
He will not see me stopping here
To watch his woods fill up with snow.

My little horse must think it queer
To stop without a farmhouse near
Between the woods and frozen lake
The darkest evening of the year.

He gives his harness bells a shake
To ask if there is some mistake.
The only other sound's the sweep
Of easy wind and downy flake.

The woods are lovely, dark, and deep,
But I have promises to keep,
And miles to go before I sleep,
And miles to go before I sleep.

~ Robert Frost (1874 - 1963)

Grandson Brad Edwards and friend Keegan Yates

AS WHITE AS SNOW

As evidenced in the photo, you can tell that our grandson, Brad, loves snow. It is a rare occasion that does not find him barefoot or wearing flip-flops, no matter how frigid the weather.

Brad attended Michigan Technological University which has a multitude of outdoor sports including ice hockey, figure skating and snowmobiling. They also have a winter carnival which features human ice bowling, snowshoe races, the human sled dog race, and other fun events. Brad was involved in broomball, which is similar to hockey, but instead of wearing ice skates, participants wear sneakers. Even though we live in Southern Illinois, we were able to watch him play through a live web cam.

I love snow. Of course, now that I'm "old" I prefer not to be out in it for long periods of time, but I still love to see soft, beautiful snowflakes gently falling from the sky. Lady Bird Johnson (1912-2007) said, *"When I no longer thrill to the first snow of the season, I'll know I'm growing old."* It has been said that snow is God's fingerprint in creation.

People love snow because it covers everything in a fresh, white blanket. Since snow is made of ice crystals, and frozen water is clear, why is snow white? The color "white" is often thought of as the absence of color, but the opposite is true. White is a combination of all the colors of the spectrum. Although difficult to explain, the whiteness of snow has something to do with the way light is reflected from one ice crystal to another, even making the snow seem to sparkle.

The color "white" in the Bible is a symbol of purity. God speaks to us in Isaiah 1:18, "...*Though your sins are like scarlet, they shall be as white as snow.*" Whether from blood, ketchup, lipstick or beet juice, the color red is one of the hardest stains to remove. But it doesn't matter whether our sins are deep red or pitch black, nothing is too hard for God. "*I am the LORD, the God of all mankind. Is anything too hard for me?*" (Jeremiah 32:27)

If we ask God to cleanse us, He will make our sins as white as snow!

PONDERINGS

~ Do you like snow? What are your favorite "snow" memories?

~ Read Mark 9:1-3. What laundry detergent do you think works best? Why does the scripture emphasize that Jesus' face and clothes were dazzling white? What truth is this vision trying to communicate?

~ Read James 2:10. Do most people tend to classify sin according to the deepness of the stain? Does this verse leave you feeling hopeless? Why or why not?

Have mercy on me, O God, according to your unfailing love; according to your great compassion blot out my transgressions. Wash away all my iniquity and cleanse me from my sin... Cleanse me with hyssop, and I will be clean; wash me, and I will be whiter than snow. Amen (Psalm 51:1-2, 7)

Photo by Fred Grayson, Poplar Bluff, MO

WHITER THAN SNOW

Lord Jesus, I long to be perfectly whole;
I want Thee forever to live in my soul;
Break down every idol, cast out every foe—
Now wash me, and I shall be whiter than snow.

Refrain:
Whiter than snow, yes, whiter than snow,
Now wash me, and I shall be whiter than snow.

Lord Jesus, look down from Thy throne in the skies,
And help me to make a complete sacrifice;
I give up myself, and whatever I know—
Now wash me, and I shall be whiter than snow.

~ *James L. Nicholson (1828-1876)*

"Elsa," photo by Katelyn Long, Marion, IL

Peace I leave with you;
my peace I give you.
I do not give to you as the world gives.
Do not let your hearts be troubled
and do not be afraid.

~ John 14:27

STRESSED OUT

Stress comes in all forms. The older my husband and I get, the more we find it stressful to travel in heavy traffic. Our memory is not as good as it used to be, so arriving at the correct destination in a timely manner can be more than challenging.

Heavy traffic is only one source of anxiety. Stress tends to appear when we are tired or sick or late for a meeting. It multiplies when we have relationship problems, when our finances are sadly lacking, or when our safety is threatened.

Our daughter, Karen, was on an airplane trip one time on a small plane when the weather turned ugly, and wind shear hit the plane. The plane was flipping back and forth like a wet rag doll. A lot of people were using the barf bags, and she heard people praying, *"Lord, don't let me die."* Karen said a quick prayer for her husband and children and then said, *"I'm OK with you, Lord, so I'm ready to die but please don't let me throw up."* The airplane was coming in for a sideways landing but the pilot was able to right the plane at the last minute for a safe landing.

What stresses out one person may not stress out another, but we are all vulnerable. What should we do when we begin to lose our peace and tranquility? We can start by setting priorities and doing only one thing at a time. The key word may be "doing." It helps when we can "do" something instead of just worrying about it. The saying is correct that *"we must stop stewing and start doing."*

On the other hand, there are also times when we must stop "doing" and start "trusting." Stress can have a positive side. It can be a reminder that we have started depending on ourselves more than on God. Jesus said in John 14:1, *"Do not let your hearts be troubled. Trust in God; trust also in me."* The dictionary says that "trust" is the *"firm belief in the reliability, truth, ability or strength of someone or something."* For the Christian, that trust must also extend to our belief that God is not only powerful, but that He cares about us. 1 Peter 5:7 tells us to... *"Cast all your anxiety on (God) because he cares for you."*

Corrie Ten Boom (1892-1983) gave us some good advice for when we are stressed out. She said, *"Never be afraid to trust an unknown future to a known God!"*

PONDERINGS

~ What images come to mind when you hear the word "stress"? What or who stresses you out the most?

~ Notice that the word "stressed" is "desserts" spelled backyards. What worldly comforts do people turn to in times of stress? Does it usually help or compound the problem?

~ Read Jeremiah 17:7-8. What is God trying to tell us about stress?

O Christ Jesus, when all is darkness and we feel our weakness and helplessness, give us the sense of Your presence, Your love, and Your strength. Help us to have perfect trust in Your protecting love and strengthening power, so that nothing may frighten or worry us, for, living close to You, we shall see Your hand, Your purpose, Your will through all things. Amen.

~ St. Ignatius of Loyola (1491-1556)

> Give thanks to the LORD,
> for he is good.
> "His love endures forever."
>
> Psalm 136:1

Photo by Christina White, Grand Rapids, MI

A GOD THING

My friend, Kim Swinford, in Marion, Illinois, shares the following story:

I wanted to share this morning that I'm smiling with joy about God's goodness! Riley, my oldest son (19 years old) called me late last night about 11:30 on his way home. He wanted to tell me about his day (doesn't happen too often). When I saw it was him calling that late, my heart raced. I anxiously said "Hello?" but could tell instantly by his tone that he was ok.

He started by saying, "*Mom, I wanted to tell you that I had a God thing happen to me today.*" He then went on excitedly to share his good news on how God had provided the right person just at the right time to help him when he needed it.

He said "*I didn't know how I was going to do it and was sitting worrying when my phone rang and then I had the answer and it was even more than I needed...it was a God thing!*" I said as only a mom would, "*Did you take time to thank God?*"

"*Oh - Like about a 100 times!*" Riley laughed.

I hope he could tell that I was smiling and choking back tears at the same time as my heart swelled with joy. As a mother, it's always good to hear that the things you have taught your children are there when they need them and to see the fruits of your labors when they grow up.

God is Good! Even when my teenager calls to tell me late at night! God's word says it best: Proverbs 22:6, *"Train up a child in the way he should go and he will not depart from it."*

We rejoice when we hear stories like Kim's because we all need to be reminded of how often in our daily lives we encounter a *God thing*. Many times, we take the *God things* in our lives for granted. Most of the time, however, we are simply unobservant or too preoccupied to recognize that the wonderful blessings coming our way could ONLY be from God.

Many years ago, I attended a women's seminar led by Jill Briscoe, who is an international Bible teacher. She encouraged us to go on a daily *God-hunt* to see where God's Hand was moving in our ordinary circumstances.

How did Riley learn to recognize and appreciate a *God thing* in his life? Knowing Kim as I do, I'm positive it was NOT because she preached to him 24/7. More than likely, he learned it from observing her daily choices, and the amount of emphasis she placed on spiritual values. He learned to truly appreciate *a God thing*!

PONDERINGS

~ How do you answer those who say, *"If God is good, why does he allow suffering?"*

~ Have you had any *God things* happen in your life? Explain.

~ Read Psalm 34:8. How do we *taste and see* that God is good?

For all Thy gifts we bless Thee, Lord, but chiefly for our heavenly food; Thy pardoning grace, Thy quickening word, These prompt our song that God is good. Amen. ~ John H. Gurney (1827-1844)

Grandson Joseph Montoya, Yukon, OK

DON'T LET ANYONE GET YOUR GOAT

The phrase, "get your goat," refers to an old belief that keeping a goat in the barn had a calming effect on cows, making them produce more milk. To antagonize the enemy, one would steal their goat, making their cows produce less milk. The theory was that if you did not want anyone to get your goat, you would not tell them where it was tied up. The real meaning was that if another person did not know your weaknesses, they would not be able to use them against you.

What are the things that "get your goat"? Here are some common ones: displays of selfishness, disrespect for your property, spreading rumors, telling lies, ignoring you and even the habits of other drivers in traffic. But one thing that easily pops to the front of the list is when someone criticizes what you do. We immediately bristle and begin to defend ourselves. The following anonymous quote gives us some great advice: *"Don't mind criticism. If it is untrue, disregard it; if unfair, keep from irritation; if it is ignorant, smile; if it is justified it is not criticism, learn from it."*

"If it is justified"... It is not easy to take a long, hard look at ourselves and admit that the unpleasant things being said about us may be grounded in truth. It is even more difficult for us to swallow our pride and use that information to begin positive changes in our behavior. The bottom line is that no one can upset us without our permission. Eleanor Roosevelt said, *"No one can make you feel inferior without your consent."*

When someone tries to get our goat, our reaction should be one of love and forgiveness. Life is too short to give in to bitterness, and if we do give in, life may become even shorter. Internal anger can affect our health. Anger affects the heart, the digestive system and the immune system. It can lead to stroke, heart disease, ulcers and some cancers. Nelson Mandela (1918-2013) said, *"Resentment is like drinking poison and hoping it will kill your enemies."*

Ephesians 4:31 says, *"Don't let anyone get your goat."* Actually, that is my personal interpretation of, *"Get rid of all bitterness, rage and anger, brawling and slander, along with every form of malice."* You will be blessed if you do.

PONDERINGS

~ What ticks you off the most? Do you become upset more easily or less easily as you become older?

~ Read Colossians 3:12-13. Is this easier said than done? What part of this verse hits home the most?

~ What if you don't really feel like doing these things? Should you just fake it?

O God, you have bound us together in a common life. Help us, in the midst of our struggles for justice and truth, to confront one another without hatred or bitterness, and to work together with mutual forbearance and respect; through Jesus Christ our Lord. Amen. ~ 1928 Book of Common Prayer

Killdeer, Lake Whippoorwill, Marion, IL

COURAGE

The Killdeer is a bird that is named for its song: *"Kill-dee, kill-dee, kill-dee."* It is part of the Plover family, has long legs and runs more than it flies.

During her evening jog, our grandson's wife, Courtney, discovered a Killdeer's nest about ½ mile from our home. There were four beautiful speckled eggs in the nest, and we checked on them daily hoping to get a glimpse of the babies. The nests are always built out in an open area, but the speckled eggs are difficult to see among the rocks. Unlike most birds, both Mommy and Daddy share the responsibility of sitting on the eggs. Mrs. Killdeer sits on the nest during the day, and Mr. Killdeer sits on it at night.

When we approached the nest, Mrs. Killdeer exhibited a spastic dance and a "broken wing display" while squealing loudly, trying desperately to lead us away from the nest. If we ignored her dramatics and walked toward the nest, she would bravely come within inches of us, loudly rebelling at our intrusion. To Mrs. Killdeer, we were the giants in the land, but she did not hesitate to confront us in order to protect her unborn chicks, showing no concern for her own safety. That's the way mamas are!

The amount of courage we have at any given moment may depend on one of two things. 1) How much the outcome matters. (When it comes to the safety of their children, parents care immensely about the outcome.) 2) How much confidence we have in victory. For the Christian, our confidence does not come from our own strength or expertise. It comes from our faith in a loving God. *"But thanks be to God! He gives us the victory through our Lord Jesus Christ."* (1 Corinthians 15:57)

There are many times in life when we need to summon our courage, in spite of our fear, and go forward against the odds. According to Nelson Mandela (1918-2013), *"...courage is not the absence of fear, but the triumph over it. The brave man is not he who does not feel afraid, but he who conquers that fear."* Thomas Edison (1847-1931) gave us this advice: *"Be courageous! Have faith! Go forward!"*

The Bible gives us advice as well: *"Be strong and courageous. Do not be afraid or terrified because of them, for the LORD your God goes with you; he will never leave you nor forsake you."* (Deuteronomy 31:6)

PONDERINGS

~ What is your favorite Bible story about courage? How does it inspire you?

~ Read Isaiah 41:10. Give an example of a situation when God gave you courage?

~ Change takes courage. Name two things in your life that will take courage to change.

God of our life, there are days when...the road seems dreary and endless...when our lives have no music in them...and our souls have lost their courage. Flood the path with light, we beseech Thee; turn our eyes to where the skies are full of promise; tune our hearts to brave music. Amen.   ~ St. Augustine (354-430)

Idella
Edwards

Idella Edwards

Idella Edwards

Idella Edwards

Idella
Edwards

COURAGE

Courage is accepting humility.
Courage is choosing the other path.
Courage is standing up for the weak.
Courage is being kind to the defenseless.
Courage is what it takes to be different.
Courage is choosing right over wrong.

It's choosing to be your own self.
It's not doing what the world does.
It's being kind to those who are hurting.
It's helping those who are taunted.
It's listening to the cry of the poor.
It's loving your enemies, not hating.

Do you have what it takes?
Are you strong enough?
Do you have the courage
To go against the flow?

Courage.

~ Granddaughter Jackie Edwards
(Written at age 13)

CONCLUSION

We sometimes lose hope and hang our harps on the willow tree, but God doesn't want us to leave them there. Ephesians 1:18 tells us that He has called us to hope: *"I pray also that the eyes of your heart may be enlightened in order that you may know the hope to which he has called you..."* My prayer is that at least one of these devotionals has inspired the eyes of your heart to be enlightened and deep inside, your hope will begin to flourish and grow.

In the prayer below, Sir Francis Drake asks God to *"...push back the horizons of our hopes; and to push into the future in strength, courage, hope, and love."* We tend to limit hope to our human understanding instead of expanding our horizons to match God's unlimited power and love.

DISTURB US, O LORD

Disturb us, O Lord, when we are too well pleased with ourselves, when our dreams have come true because we have dreamed too little, when we arrive safely because we have sailed too close to the shore.

Disturb us, O Lord, when with the abundance of things we possess, we have lost our thirst for the waters of life; having fallen in love with life, we have ceased to dream of eternity; and in our efforts to build a new earth, we have allowed our vision of the new Heaven to dim.

Disturb us, O Lord, to dare more boldly, to venture on wider seas where storms will show your mastery; where losing sight of land, we shall find the stars. We ask you to push back the horizons of our hopes; and to push into the future in strength, courage, hope, and love.

~ Sir Frances Drake (1540 - 1596)

Hope can be elusive. Life has the ability to crush our hopes with a single devastating blow. It could be the result of a financial burden, a health issue or a destroyed relationship, but the disappearance of hope can threaten to destroy our very lives. The empty tomb gives us hope - not only the hope of eternal life, but the hope and assurance that God cares about every detail of our lives. We have no reason to hang our harps on the willow tree. Our God is a God of hope! *"For I know the plans I have for you," declares the LORD, "plans to prosper you and not to harm you, plans to give you hope and a future."* (Jeremiah 29:11)

When we are tempted to lose hope, we must remember ONE thing. God is bigger than our problems. He is everything we will ever need in this life and the next.

LORD, YOU ARE

When my last ounce of energy has drained away
And my body is weary at the end of the day,
Lord, YOU are my Strength!

When I'm totally lost with no end in sight,
Wandering aimlessly all through the night,
Lord, YOU are my Way!

When my heart is heavy and life gets me down,
The tears overflow and my face wears a frown,
Lord, YOU are my Joy!

When the valleys are low and the mountains are high,
When my soul is discouraged and it's useless to try,
Lord, YOU are my Hope!

When things unexplained go bump in the night,
And the lurking shadows give me a fright
Lord, YOU are my Peace!

When life hands out lemons and I'm tired of the games,
When all of my efforts go up in flames,
Lord, YOU are my Everything!

~ *Idella Pearl Edwards*

Don't hang your harps on the willow tree! If you have lost sight of the great hope we have in Christ, go to God. Ask him to restore your hope. He is able to pour His hope into our lives. Romans 15:13 talks about overflowing with hope. If we are so full of hope that we overflow, it will spill out into the lives of our friends and family and neighbors.

Hope is based on faith. We will never be able to wait patiently for something we don't believe is going to happen.

God makes a promise.
Faith believes it.
Hope anticipates it.
Patience quietly awaits it.

~ Anonymous

I am praying for you as you renew your hope and faith in the Almighty God of the Universe. *"And hope does not disappoint us, because God has poured out his love into our hearts by the Holy Spirit, whom he has given us."* (Romans 5:5)

God Bless!
Idella

Hope is the only bee that makes honey without flowers.

~ Robert Ingersoll
(1833-1899)

Becki Flood, Moore, OK, 1973

Shout for joy to the LORD, all the earth,
burst into jubilant song with music;
make music to the LORD with the harp,
with the harp and the sound of singing,
with trumpets and the blast of the ram's horn –
shout for joy before the LORD, the King.

~ Psalm 98:4-6

INDEX OF POETRY AND LYRICS

The Willow Tree	3
Hope	7
My Shadow	8
This World Is Not My Home	11
Will Jesus Find Us Watching?	15
How Firm A Foundation	20
My Hope Is Built On Nothing Less	23
God's Gift Of Family	37
Choose To Be Happy	41
The Big Yellow Book	42
Love Letter From God	45
Oft In Danger, Oft In Woe	49
To God Be The Glory	50
Listen To Wisdom	54
How Fleeting My Life	69
Come, Holy Spirit, Lord, Our God	70
Send The Fire	73
The Sunflower Surprise	74
The Butterfly	82
Open My Eyes, That I May See	86
We Must Get Home	90
Home! Sweet Home!	93
God's World Of Flowers	94
Allegories Of Forgiveness	98
The Little Bench	101
The Cross	102
The Love Of God	105
Come To The Table	113
Let There Be Light	114
O Jesus, Lord Of Light And Grace	117
The Gift Of Music	120
God Gives A Song	123
This Day	124
This Day At Thy Creating Word	127
Wholeness	128
Things To Remember	132

The Bumblebee	142
What A Baby Costs	150
Prayer	161
Celebrate	162
The Road Not Taken	166
I Am The Door	170
God Stills The Storm	179
Stopping By Woods On A Snowy Evening	180
Whiter Than Snow	183
Courage	194
Lord, You Are	196

What gives me the most hope
every day is God's grace;
knowing that his grace is going
to give me the strength for whatever I face,
knowing that nothing is a surprise to God.

~ Rick Warren

ACKNOWLEDGMENTS

PROOFING: A debt of gratitude goes to husband, Jack Edwards and daughter, Rhonda Andersen for their expertise and tireless dedication in proofing my book. Thanks also to my family and friends for their warm words of encouragement.

PHOTOGRAPHY: Grateful appreciation is extended to the following photographers who, in addition to my own, generously shared their photos.

David Andersen, Marion, IL (grandson)
James Andersen, Marion, IL (son-in-law)
Danielle Barter, Johnston City, IL (friend)
Melissa Chaussé, Marion, IL (friend)
Rev. Stan Cosby, Amarillo, TX (friend)
Courtney Edwards, Murphysboro, IL (grandson's wife)
Bruce Edwards, Bloomfield, IN (son)
Jack Edwards, Marion, IL (husband)
John and Colleen Eisenberg, Asunción, Paraguay (friends)
Fred Grayson, Poplar Bluff, MO (friend)
Allen Gibbs, Chester, IL (friend)
Janet Hatfield, Middletown, IN (friend)
Brian Jennings, Pittsburgh, PA (friend)
Ken Johnson, Aurora, IL (friend)
Tauna Kobler, Marion, IL (friend)
Laura Lovell, Oklahoma City, OK (friend)
Debbie Martin, Dickinson, TX (friend)
Karen Malone, Fenton, MO (daughter)
Kerry Jo Montoya, Yukon, OK (daughter)
Ziden Nutt, Carthage, MO (cousin)
Rebecca Odle, Marion, IL (friend)
Sylvia Petrey, Norman, OK (friend)
Liz Reynolds, Marion, IL (friend)
Joshua Roman, Oklahoma City, OK (friend)
William Van Atte, Batchawana Bay, ON (cousin)
Kim Vanderhelm, Allendale, MI (friend)
Christina White, Grand Rapids, MI (friend)

POETRY: I would like to thank all of my poet friends who graciously allowed the use of their poetry for my book.

Jackie Edwards (granddaughter)
Sharon Hubbell (friend)
Sarah Martin (friend)
Bridget Rossi (friend)

PUBLIC DOMAIN IMAGES - All photos and images not otherwise identified are in the public domain.

Rainbow, Costa Rica
Photo by William E. Van Atte, Batchawana Bay, ON

God puts rainbows in the clouds
so that each of us —
in the dreariest
and most dreaded moments —
can see a possibility of HOPE.

~ Maya Angelou

ABOUT THE AUTHOR

Idella Edwards retired from the State of Oklahoma in 2005 but has also lived in eight different states. She currently resides in Marion, Illinois where she is an active member of Aldersgate United Methodist Church, team-teaching an adult Sunday School class, singing in the choir, participating in United Methodist Women and leading a group called Body & Soul. In addition to writing books, she is also a published poet and newspaper columnist.

Born and raised in Aurora, Illinois, Idella attended Olivet Nazarene University and received a degree from College of DuPage. She and her husband, Jack, have five children and twelve grandchildren. They spent several years coordinating Lay Witness Missions and have been Certified Lay Speakers for the United Methodist Church since 1990.

Previous publications include, "HOPE, Through Eyes Of Faith," "MAGNIFY, Inspirational Poetry for the Soul," "RESPECT FOR PARENTS 101, From A Grandmother's Point Of View," and "LOOK AT THE BIRDS, God's Love Revealed Through Nature."

CPSIA information can be obtained
at www.ICGtesting.com
Printed in the USA
FSHW010108040621
81961FS